50 Days for Fifty Years
Walking the Camino de Santiago

Blaise van Hecke

All truly great thoughts are conceived while walking.
— Friedrich Nietzsche

First published by Pinion Press 2020
Copyright © 2020 Blaise van Hecke
Paperback: 978-1-925949-60-5
Ebook: 978-1-925949-61-2

All rights reserved. No part of this publication may be reproduced, stored in or introduced into a retrieval system, or transmitted in any form, or by any means (electronic, mechanical, photocopying, recording or otherwise) without the prior written permission of the author. Any person who does any unauthorised act in relation to this publication may be liable to criminal prosecution and civil claims for damages. Enquiries should be made through the publisher.

Pinion Press is an imprint of Busybird Publishing
www.busybird.com.au

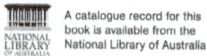

To Kev,
the best travel partner for thirty-three years

and Dylan & Jack,
may your life be one big adventure.

When I was thirty-five, one of my yoga buddies was turning fifty. Instead of a big party, she planned to meet her daughter, who lived in London, in the south of France to walk the Camino de Santiago. I'd never heard of it but loved the idea and filed it away thinking that I would do the same. It was a long way off: turning fifty.

The Camino de Santiago is an ancient pilgrim walk across the north of Spain. Traditionally it starts in Saint Jean Pied de Port (SJPP) in France and travels along the Way of Saint James, under the stars (the Milky Way), over the Pyrenees into Spain for eight hundred kilometres to the Cathedral in Santiago where the body of the Apostle Saint James is said to be interred. Legend says that in 813 a shepherd named Pelayo was drawn to a field in Libredon (now Santiago) by a bright light or star (compostela). The pilgrim walk is often referred to as Santiago de Compostela because of this. The Bishop of Pedron declared that the body of Saint James was entombed in this field and the Cathedral of Santiago now houses this tomb.

The Camino de Santiago is one of many spiritual pilgrimages in the world. Between the twelfth and fourteenth centuries it was prestigious. This popularity declined, but over the last twenty years it has had a resurgence and more and more people are making this pilgrimage.

Yellow arrows and scallop shells show the pilgrim the Way and pilgrim hostels called "albergues" give refuge after a long day of walking. At each albergue, when you check in, your credential is stamped and you are given a bed and sometimes a pilgrim meal.

Over the years the Camino kept popping up to remind me of that pledge I'd made to myself. Then I met a woman, Marg, who wanted to publish her book about her own pilgrim walk.[1] The universe was not going to let me forget the promise I'd made.

Before I knew it, my fiftieth birthday loomed. I started saying half-heartedly that I was going to walk that ancient pilgrim path – the Way – but I didn't actually believe it. I'm a small business owner; there was no way I could take off six or seven weeks to do something like that.

Or could I?

The pull was strong and once I voiced that I DID want to do this, everything conspired to help me make

---

1 *Walking Back Home* by Margaret Caffyn

it happen. Enter a supportive partner, fabulous family and friends.

Everything moved fast in the lead up to the trip and suddenly I was on board the plane bound for Madrid, Spain. I was filled with a mix of excitement and anxiety. For the first time in my life I was heading overseas on my own for seven weeks.

please note that all distances are approximate. I found distances to be fluid on the Camino de Santiago.

Sunday 15 April: Melbourne to Madrid via Abu Dhabi, 17,285 kms

I am delirious by the time I land in Madrid; I've never been able to sleep well on a plane. But catching the train from Madrid airport is easier than I expect, then only a couple of stops to Gran Via where Praktik Metropol is. There it is, perched up against McDonalds. My room is on the fourth floor. I *was* hoping for a view of Madrid (never trust the photos on the net) but the room is cute with black and white checkered tiles on the bathroom floor.

A room of my own.

I peel off my trusty green hiking boots, merino socks and hiking clothes. I wore my boots on the plane in case my bag went missing.

I have a shower to wash away the hours of travel, then walk around the streets to get my bearings. I am fluttery with excitement and can't believe I'm here. I buy a SIM card at Vodafone, feeling awkward and self-conscious about being a foreigner without much Spanish and the girl serving me isn't exactly friendly.[2]

---

2 SIM card for 28 days, €20

I wonder if this will be typical of Spaniards.

There are hours until dinner so I admire the crisp white sheets on my bed. It's time to have a nap but I've realised that my phone charger has the wrong connection for Spain and the power is low. I head out to the shops. They're closed. Siesta time.

I FaceTime with Kev and Jack to show them my room. I'm on such a high, on the brink of a girls' own adventure. I'm not sure they share my love of the room or the tiny cupboard-sized bathroom but they are happy for me. I lie on the clean white sheets and close my eyes.

I wake at eight, groggy. The long flight has taken its toll. I spill out onto the plaza outside my hotel. It's packed with Sunday strollers, walking arm-in-arm. The springtime sun is gentle and I almost expect to get a whiff of a sea breeze; the promenade of holidaymakers.

I find a table for one at a nearby restaurant and order lasagna.[3] The menu is limited and so far I'm not impressed with the food. I leave feeling bloated. I'm not sure what time my body thinks it is.

I fall back into bed around ten and sleep fitfully in the over-hot room.

---

3 Dinner with wine €12

1 Monday 16 April: Madrid to Saint Jean Pied de Port (SJPP), 467kms

I can't sleep. I turn on the bedside lamp at four to check the train schedule for Pamplona. I gasp. The only train this morning is at seven-thirty. I need to take a morning train in order to get the connecting bus over the mountain to my starting point in Saint Jean Pied de Port (France).

I bolt out of bed, pack my bright blue backpack and dash out into the street. I'm grateful for a good train system that is easy to navigate even in a foreign tongue. I get to the ticketing booth at six-thirty. There are only first class tickets left; I berate myself for not booking weeks ago back in Australia but I wanted this trip to be as unplanned as possible. This is what you get.[4]

After buying my ticket I have twenty minutes to wait. I grab a coffee and pastry for breakfast and sit to watch Spaniards dashing past to catch their trains, while I eat.

I'm not sure what the difference is for first class. It

---

[4] First class train Madrid to Pamplona €80 (more than twice the cost of second class)

seems the same as any other train trip but I'm keen to see the countryside and it's disappointing that there isn't much to look at for the next three hours.

The train arrives in Pamplona and I tumble out, lugging my backpack. I feel conspicuous and self-conscious on my own. Using mime and a few badly pronounced Spanish words, I find myself on a bus heading for the central bus station where I buy a ticket to Saint Jean Pied de Port.[5]

Now what? There are hours to go before the bus leaves. I'm tired and hungry and I haven't even started yet.

I walk a few blocks, still lugging all my belongings, looking at menus and restaurants to work out what to eat. I'm hesitant to go into any in case I don't like the food or draw too much attention to myself. My self-talk is impatient.

Just choose a damn place to eat!

I walk into a café that is bustling. I feel awkward with my luggage. Maybe I should have gotten a locker at the station to store it? But it's warm in here and the food looks okay. I order potato frittata and decadent hot chocolate that is so thick I almost can't drink it. The sugar bolsters me.[6]

---
5 Pastry and coffee at train station €3; local bus €1.20; bus to SJPP €24
6 Lunch €7

Finally, the bus. A line of pilgrims (evident by luggage and attire) waddles onto the bus bound for the Pyrenees. Eyes dart everywhere as people check each other out – what they are wearing, how much they are carrying, comparing, evaluating.

As we make our way up the mountain the anticipation grows. The scenery is lush, green, gorgeous. Am I actually here? Fifteen years of manifestation? This is where I'll be walking tomorrow! It's strange to be going to SJPP, then to walk back over the mountain on foot but that's what I'll be doing. I chat with an American woman next to me but I don't think I'm listening. To be honest I wish I could sit with my thoughts.

At four-fifteen we arrive. The Pilgrim welcome office is easy to find – just follow the pilgrims! I'm the only one in the office on rue de la Citadelle when I register and I suddenly feel emotion well up in me. This is getting real and I'm here all on my own.

Clutching my Pilgrim passport, I walk up the tiny cobbled street to the albergue, Les Amis de la Vielle Navarre, where I get my pilgrim passport stamped for the first time and get assigned the top bunk – number 116 (E10).[7] I dump my pack next to the bunk, then wonder what to do.

It's cool so I don my beanie and walk the streets to

---

7 Pilgrim passport €5; albergue €10

get some bearings. I have been transported back in time to this gorgeous medieval city that was once a gateway for travellers – and I guess still is. I walk around the Citadelle up on the hill, which gives me a great view of the city and a chance for a selfie.

I am yet to feel comfortable on my own. I'm so used to company when I travel but I can see there are many other pilgrims who are on their own. I sit in the albergue kitchen and talk with other pilgrims sitting at the table. I'm surprised by how intimate the conversations are when we're essentially strangers. I see a pattern to the order of questions:

Where are you from?
How old are you?
Why are you walking?
How far are you walking?
Are you solo?

One of the top reasons for walking – feeling lost. One man, Julio (American from Argentina), who must be around seventy years old, is meeting up with his female friend from Denmark. He's on his fourth Camino, she on her ninth! They met when he was on his first and have walked it together every year since. In his words, 'For one month we are in love.' He watches the time incessantly, and then disappears down the hill to pick her up from the bus station.

Another man, a German, thirty-two years old, is walking because he feels lost. He's happily married with a young daughter. His life is good but something is missing. His pain is palpable. I hope he finds what he's looking for.

I mostly listen to people. I'm not sure why I'm here. It sounds shallow to be walking just to celebrate turning fifty.

I have my first pilgrim meal as suggested by Julio at a tavern down the street. Vegetable soup, chicken and potato, followed by apple crumble. I can't eat the dessert so I stow it away for later.[8] I'll appreciate that tomorrow.

I'd like to say I fall into bed but I am on the top bunk. I clamber up to it and shuffle into my sleeping bag. It's been a big day and tomorrow I start.

Love is a new adventure.

---

8 Pilgrim meal €9

2 Tuesday 17 April: Saint Jean Pied de Port to Orisson, 8kms

And so it begins … an early start thanks to a bad night's sleep – the room is too hot and there was a chorus of snorers – and then a room full of people packing their bags from five-thirty. It's dark and cold outside and I'm reluctant to start.

I put on all my cold weather clothes because I know it's about one degree Celsius outside. I eat some of the complimentary breakfast and I'm out the door by seven-fifty and weighed down by the fog. Within ten minutes I'm stripping off as the fog burns away to a glorious sunny day.

Oh my, what scenery. Blue, clear skies with hawks circling above and mist rising in wafts. I say hello to a pony in a paddock and marvel at the lifting vapor as it weaves a magic spell over the land. I'm walking along a country laneway in France on my own. I'm talking to myself. A lot. This morning it's *nice* talk.

The nice talk turns to pain and moaning. The road climbs abruptly and the angle is steep. I stop. Walk. Stop. My pack is like a deadweight and I already wish

I had a smaller one. I'm only a few kilometres into my pilgrim walk and I'm in pain. How will I do this for eight hundred more kilometres? I also wonder where the "790 Santiago" sign is. Kev had bossed me about getting a picture of myself with it but I haven't seen it.

Behind me, an older woman jabbers on her mobile phone. She's obviously a pilgrim but her clothes are more eccentric and she has a wooden staff instead of walking poles. Her talking on the phone is annoying me. I sit to rest and silently berate her. Then I see Julio is with her and realise this must be his Danish friend. She's wearing lipstick!

I keep walking. Or maybe you could call it *crawling*. Marg had warned me about this first day and that it would be one of my most difficult days.

At eleven-thirty I round a curve in the road and behold Albergue Orisson.[9] An oasis. It's so good to stop and have a fresh OJ and a jambon and frommage sandwich, which is a baguette. It's too big to eat so I've saved half for the road tomorrow. I check into the room – six people in bunks. We sit out on the deck for hours enjoying the gentle sun and those spectacular views, talking about anything and everything. Julio and the Dane stop for a while, but then keep walking.

I have a shower and wash my hair with the soap bar

---

9 On advice from Marg, I pre-booked this night from Australia for €35

(honey scented) that I bought for the trip, then use it to wash my socks and undies.[10] It works better than I expected.

Dinner is at six-thirty: veggie soup, pork and beans, then rice pudding. Wine comes with it but it's not great. Everyone has to stand and introduce themselves and tell us why they are doing the Camino: so many retired or between jobs.

I sit near a retired couple from Argentina. Their English is basic but they manage to communicate so well despite it. They are using trolleys to cart their gear along the Way because they feel too old to carry a pack. The husband has made them himself and beams with pride.

Love is the view from Orisson over the French Alps.

---

10 Lush solid soap bar. This bar lasted my whole trip. The honey smells lovely and is antibacterial

3 Wednesday 18 April: Orisson to Roncesvalles, 17.5kms

I sleep soundly from nine until six. This is unusual for me. I have trouble getting to sleep and if I wake during the night, I need to start the whole 'get to sleep' process again. I guess the walking exhausted me.

Complimentary breakfast is at seven – a bowl of coffee – with a vivid sunrise over the Pyrenees.

The wind is icy cold on my face but a clear blue sky hangs overhead as I trudge up the mountain. About halfway up there sits a food van. I buy a banana and sit, my face feeling skinless from the wind.[11] A young Australian man stops for a break. He slings his pack onto the ground and nods hello. I overhear him talking to someone nearby. He's walked from SJPP this morning – easily twelve kilometres and it's only ten am. I deflate as he hikes onwards five minutes later.

Seemingly in the middle of nowhere I come across a statue that looks to be ceramic. This is at Pic D'Orisson (1,100 metres). The statue of the virgin set against the

---

11 A Camino banana costs €1

backdrop of the mountains and valleys is surreal. A selfie is in order.

There are patches of pure white snow at the edges of the pathways and crystal clear water melting and trickling away from it. Birds always chirping. There are moments of tranquility out of the wind when walking though the forests. The witches of the past peer out at me. A scattering of white pebbles on the ground amongst the trees gets my imagination fired up. There is history and secrets spirited here.

Other pilgrims stream past me but I'm determined to walk at a turtle pace. This is rewarded when I spot the tiniest bat hanging upside down on a barbed wire fence. I get my new camera out and take lots of photos on macro while still carrying my pack. It's hard to squat and balance like this but there is nowhere to put my pack – only slushy mud everywhere. A breeze skips past and history whispers to me.

Finally I reach the top of the mountain and drop to the ground behind a hut to get out of the bitter wind. I'm exhausted. I sit for a while enjoying the spectacular views and take my socks off and eat my 'sandwich'.

I pass over into Spain and am now in Navarre. This is a relatively pleasant flat pathway. I take my time, stopping often to drink water or sit by the pathway.

Once I start the downhill descent, I realise that up isn't so bad, it's the downhill on the last four kilometres that gets me. My knees complain and I'm glad to have the walking poles that I had actually considered not bringing.[12]

What a long day! I finally approach Roncevalles and its HUGE monastery at around three-thirty.[13] There is a stream of pilgrims. I'm not sure where they've all come from because it wasn't that busy along the Way. I am happy to be given my bed and I'm determined to keep the bottom bunk despite some young Italian men trying to trick me out of it. They don't understand that I'm old and cynical and their Italian charm won't work on me.

I FaceTime with Kev. It's the first time since I started walking that I've had Internet. Poor thing is stressed about running the business. I'm not much use from so far away but I'm sure he'll work it out.

I have a lovely long hot shower and am almost human after that. The rooms are big and full of cubicles, each with two bunks. I have no idea how many people it houses but there must be close to one hundred people over a few floors. It's new and is overheated but it's good to stop.

I'm too exhausted to look around, so I lie on my bed and wait for dinner at seven – vegetable soup, red wine,

---

12 Walking poles 600grams
13 Bed in 2-bunk cubicle €12, includes breakfast

pork, potatoes and strawberry yogurt. Everything but the pork is good. Baguette with everything! I sit on a table with six other pilgrims from all over the world. We share our life stories. Time moves fast.

I go to mass at eight but sneak out when they do communion. It's cold in the church and everything is in Spanish.

I can't wait to go to bed at nine. Everything aches. The lights switch off at ten – a blessing because there are so many young, chatty people that would talk and laugh into the night if they could.

And then the snoring starts.

Love is the blessing of a witch's forest.

4 Thursday 19 April: Roncesvalles to Zubiri, 21.9kms

The lights come on again at six and we file out to breakfast by seven, basically herded out of the building. I'm ready to start walking at eight but thought I'd better FaceTime Kev to give him some strategies. The call drains my phone battery. The negative thoughts crowd in, *I'm selfish for doing this.*

Then there's the sign: *Santiago de Compostella 790*. I wish Kev were here to tell him. I'm happy because I thought I'd missed it, so I take a selfie so I don't get in trouble. I'm confused by distance though. I've now walked about twenty-five kilometres and yet there's still seven hundred and ninety to go?

After the last two days of walking, this stage is pleasant. Some up and down but not as strenuous as yesterday. I make a point of stopping every hour or so. This is easy because there are gorgeous streams and meadows with cows clanking their bells. It's lovely to sit by the babbling water, it could be in Australia.

I pass a fourteenth century pilgrim cross, Cruz Peregrino. Nearby is dense woodland where secret

covens were held in the sixteenth century giving it the name 'Oakwood of Witches'.

This means that it's about four-thirty by the time I get to Zubiri. The last two hours are a struggle as I navigate the steep descent. This is the most kilometres that I've walked so far in one day. Every muscle hurts but I was like this last night then was fine by morning.

Albergue Zubiri, El Palo de Avellano, isn't bad and I get the bottom bunk again.[14] I can't face more pork, which is on the pilgrim menu, so I walk around town and hook up with other pilgrims: the couple from Argentina (I sat next to them at Orisson for dinner), a young Australian and a French girl.

I'm so hungry and eat more than I should, enjoying the company in the late evening sun, which is warm until late.[15]

Love is sharing a meal with new friends from Argentina.

---

14 Albergue & breakfast €16
15 Meal and Coke €12

5 Friday 20 April: Zubiri to Pamplona, 20.9kms

Breakfast is never hearty but at least something to start the day with. Today it's café con leche, plain croissant and fresh orange juice. I'm on the road by about eight-fifteen.

Not far out of Zubiri I pass some of my Aussie Camino friends who are looking at an old church. It's being restored and we are given a tour. So much history!

I stop for tortilla and a rest midmorning (and a toilet stop).[16] Sitting in a café on the bank of rio Arga, is civilized. I could get used to this pilgrim thing.

I stop at Zabaldika to look at the ancient belfry at Iglesia de San Estaban and enjoy a rest in the garden amongst colourful spring flowers.

Today the walking feels arduous and by about three I've had enough although I'm not at Pamplona yet. I stop often to rest.

Finally I hit Pamplona around four. The approach to the city is to cross the Puente de Magdalena XII, then turn left on the other side of the river. I'm glad that the

---

16 Tortilla €3

German-run Casa Paderborn on the Rio Arga is not far into the city because I can't walk another ten minutes.

I have a good impression of this place. It's cheap and only four to the room.[17] Bottom bunk again. One of the nuns says my bag is too heavy for me.[18] I wonder what I can offload. I don't think I have packed anything unnecessary. My sleeping bag alone weighs about eight hundred grams.

I'm unpacking, in walks Edda. I met her at Orisson on Tuesday at the group dinner. She's also walking on her own after her son did the Camino a few years ago and suggested she do it too. We decide to share a washing load since each of us doesn't have much to wash.

After a shower I decide I should look around, and I need to find dinner, so I walk into the city centre. Walking without my pack and with my sandals on is strangely less exhausting. I find it weird that I was in Pamplona waiting for a bus only a few days ago.

I'm thankful that there is no running of the bulls right now.

I do the tourist thing and seek out Plaza del Castillo with its covered arcades shading shops, bars and cafes. I find the Art Deco Café Iruna with its shiny brass

---

17 Albergue & breakfast €10
18 At this stage it was around 8 kilograms

surfaces, where Ernest Hemingway used to hang out but decide against eating here because it's expensive.

It's a lovely balmy Friday evening and families are out in the plaza. Kids chase birds and people are chattering.

Everywhere that I turn, there are so many food choices that I'm overwhelmed and can't decide what to eat. It's awkward being alone. Finally, after berating myself for not being decisive, I pick a restaurant in the middle of one of the many squares and sit down. I eat a big bowl of pasta – I've chosen a pilgrim meal, forgetting that there are three courses and I can barely finish the first. I sit and watch the masses of people jostling past and bask in the fading day.[19]

I walk too much and my joints ache. I'm homesick and missing my boys and wonder what I'm doing here and how I can make my backpack lighter.

The malaise is eased when Edda and I get our clothes – clean and folded perfectly – from the German nuns.[20]

Our other roommates arrive late – one man from Germany who walks for two weeks every year and fasts (no food and only water) while he's doing it, the other a young man (about 19, I think) from Hungary, also walking on his own to help his depression.

---

19 Pilgrim meal €20 and far too much food
20 My share for washing was €3.50

The room is small with nowhere but the bunk to sit on, so I snuggle into my sleeping bag, every muscle aching.

I'm fast asleep by ten.

Love is clean clothes.

6

Saturday 21 April: Pamplona to Obanos, 21.6kms

We are woken by singing. At first I think it's live music but soon realise it's a recording of nuns singing German songs. I have no idea what they're about but it's not a bad way to wake up.

I FaceTime with Kev bright and early and, with luck, both Dylan and Jack are also home. Talking to them relieves my homesickness.

I have breakfast in the front room with other pilgrims: coffee and white bread with jam. I'm on my way by seven-thirty. I'm refreshed but still wonder about what I can offload from my pack but there isn't anything extraneous.

Another clear, sunny day. A rhythm to each day is starting to develop although the pack is still heavy and my joints hurt. I resolve to stop every hour or so to drink water and sometimes take my boots off.[21]

I walk back through the old walled city of Pamplona, along centuries-old pavements with the shell emblem

---

21 I stop at a café for a toilet break, charge my phone, and buy a banana and apple for €1.50

to show me the way. I pass castle ruins on the right and look back over my shoulder over the wonderful views of Pamplona.

It's a long slow trudge uphill to the wind turbines and the wrought iron representation of medieval pilgrims. Alto del Perdon. The low whooshing sound of the turbines is the backing track all the way up. This is one of the landmarks that I was looking forward to and it's worth the climb.

A lot of pilgrims are walking today. Every now and again I see someone I recognise and we wave or smile at each other.

It's extremely windy up here and hard to take photos but I think I manage all right. There's a spiritual feeling at this spot and I wish it weren't so windy and noisy so that I could sit and hold the space around me. I spend most of the time trying to hold on to my hat.

The descent from there is long and steep so I stop often. I'm glad that I brought my walking poles because I don't think my knees would hold together without them.

By Uterga I'm starving so I stop at a cute café (also an albergue) and have a Coke and bowl of pasta.[22] It's easy to get caught up in the familial feel of the Camino. Wherever you stop there is likely to be other pilgrims

---

22 Lunch is €7

and it's easy to find a table with someone and share stories.

I'm tempted to stay the night here because I've been distracted by these stories and this place is inviting. But it's already three and I want to be further along my way. I'm also trying not to get too caught up in the social aspect of the walk because I'm here for myself. I want it to be as real a pilgrimage as possible.

I arrive at Obanos at five and decide that is enough for the day. The village is quiet. It's hard to believe that these places are inhabited by anyone other than pilgrims. I'm in a big albergue with not many pilgrims because most will probably be at the next town, which is more of a landmark. It's actually lovely and peaceful but cold inside Albergue Usda Obanos.[23] Thank god I still have my sleeping bag because I have been considering offloading it to reduce my weight. I like the security it gives me though, despite sometimes being too warm. There's something about crawling into a cocoon and feeling safe. I can also unzip a section at my feet if they get too hot.

There are enough beds in this room for about thirty people. There aren't many other people, but close by are two Italian couples who are travelling together. They were also at Orisson when I was there. They have loud,

---

23 Bed & breakfast is €11

animated conversations (and snore loudly too) but they are funny and friendly. One of the women loves a game on her phone that makes sounds like popping bubbles. She's obsessed with it.

I opt for a coffee and snack instead of dinner because I had a late lunch.[24]

It's barely dark when I crawl into my sleeping bag and grab the spare woolen blanket at the end of the bed in case it's cold. Despite the snoring, I fall into a sound sleep.

Love is sleeping the sleep of the dead.

---

24 Coffee & snacks €5

7 Sunday 22 April: Obanos to Villatuerta, 20.6kms

It's still dark when we gather in the cold kitchen for a pilgrim breakfast. The hospitaleria (albergue host) isn't exactly bright and chirpy but 'the Italians' are. There's plenty of food and I stash some (box juice and sweet bun) in my bag for later. I'm out with my pack by seven-thirty as the sun makes its feeble ascent into the sky. It's cold and grey but the sun sends shards of light all over the place.

As I emerge into the street outside the albergue, on the corner of the main square and San Lorenzo, I'm so much lighter then yesterday.

I stop often, especially when there's access to the river. I put my feet into the freezing cold rio Salado and the icy water shoots pain through my legs but invigorates my aching feet.

I stop to rest on an old bridge with no water under it. Since there's been so little shelter and so few places to stop I take advantage of somewhere to sit. A small group of pilgrims stops nearby and I chat to a Canadian man.

He's walking to remember his daughter, who was murdered by her partner. He's written a book about it, about forgiveness. Of course I'm interested in his story and feel the weight of it as he's talking. He leaves with his group and I'm left alone airing my hot tender feet, contemplating how much trauma people carry.

Only a few minutes further on is a gorgeous oasis amongst the trees made especially for pilgrims. It has deck chairs and juice and books to read. I wish I'd not stopped before because this would be lovely to stay at for a while.

By two, I'm tired. I'm debating with myself about my fitness. I must be crazy to think that I can do this every day for six weeks.

I arrive at Villatuerta around three, totally spent. I'm grateful that albergues are usually so easy to find. I check in to Casa Mágica to a room with only four beds, no bunks![25] When I open the door, there's Edda sitting on one of the beds. We laugh and swap Camino stories. I do some washing, shower, and talk to Kev on FaceTime. I make use of one of the sun lounges and sit in the sun for a while, then decide I need a proper lie down.

After my siesta, we go down to dinner at seven-thirty. Dinner is always so late. The food is good – one

---

25 Bed €14; dinner €13; breakfast €4.50; hot chocolate (vending machine) €1

of the better pilgrim meals: salad plus paella (I pushed aside the seafood), with wine and the best Chorizo. Then a desert-like custard. Too much food. There is plenty to talk about with my fellow pilgrims as we sit around the table.

It would be easy to do this all night but again, I'm tired. It's later than usual when I crawl into my sleeping bag at around ten.

Love is Spanish paella when you're hungry.

8

Monday 23 April: Villatuerta to Villamayor de Monjardin, 13.2kms

Despite the good food and good sleep in a single bed, my pack feels heavy. But the sun is out and it's a new day. I need to talk to Kev and put out some spot fires, so it's later than usual by the time I'm on my way.

The first two hours or so are okay; I just want to get to the wine font, *Bodegas Irache*. Finally I arrive at about ten thirty. I dig out my scallop shell to use as a cup and fill it with red wine.[26] I manage to take some photos and a live video. I'm emotional for some reason. The wine is good! Of course I'm a good girl and only take a small amount of wine. I heard they have cameras everywhere at Fuente del Vino, and only a certain amount of free wine is dispensed each day.

Despite the wine being good and feeling happy, every step is heavy; my boots aren't as light as usual. There's lots of uphill climbing and I don't think I can get far today. I arrive at Villamayor around one-forty and decide that this is it for the day.

---

26 Shell purchased in one of the towns €1.50

None of the albergues are open yet because most kick you out in the morning and then reopen after two. I choose one that's uphill and bathed in afternoon sun. It's not a bad place to wait and there are other pilgrims waiting who I can chat to. It's hot waiting, so I get a beer from the vending machine. It goes down well but straight to my head! I don't think that beer is good on an empty stomach.

Albergue Villamayor is quaint and the rooms are small with only four to six people per room.[27] I get the bottom bunk again and the room fills with five young Italian men. It heats up in the room quickly with their bodies and energy. I shower then take a walk around the town. There isn't too much to see and I'm tired.

In the evening, after dinner, we are invited to a meditation 'next door' where there is a room with cushions on the floor. The atmosphere is collegial and the mediation is relaxing. We pass an object around the room and take turns to talk about what we hope for on the Camino. I'm struck dumb when it's my turn. I feel like I should have some profound statement when there are so many pilgrims looking for something. I mumble something incoherent. I'm confused by my lack of voice in these situations.

---

27 Albergue €10; dinner €10; breakfast €5

It's dark by the time I go to bed and the view from my bunk is of the quaint church in the centre of town. I try to take some photos but my camera isn't great to hold still in low light.

I fall into deep sleep quickly.

Love is free wine.

9 Tuesday 24 April: Villamayor to Torres del Rio, 20kms

Clear blue skies again! The church bell wakes us at six in our steamy box of a room. After a quick breakfast, I'm on the Way by seven-thirty.

What a treat to leave Villamayor (Pronounce y=j) and walk on relatively flat country roads, the birds chirping all around me and every now and again a 'cuckoo, cuckoo'. Apparently, the cuckoo is prevalent around here. It's either following me or trying to tell me something. I smile every time I hear it.[28]

There aren't many people around so it's peaceful on these remote farm tracks through mixed farmland and vineyards interspersed with olive trees. The only obstacle is when a farmer comes along the track with his sheep and I have to step back into a ditch to let them bustle past me, their bleating loud so close up.

By eleven-thirty it's already warm, so I'm happy to be a few kilometres into the day already. I stop at

---

28 There's a food van with coloured plastic chairs in the middle of nowhere. I stop and buy a banana for €1 and listen to an Englishman moan and complain about other pilgrims

Los Arcos for a break and there is a group of vending machines hiding in an alcove at the outskirts of the town. I buy a Kit Kat and hot chocolate and watch pilgrims trudge by.[29]

I arrive at the town of Torres del Rio just before two. There's an old bridge over the babbling rio Linares with a quintessential pilgrim village ahead up a small hill. I can feel history here, like so many of these towns. Iglesia de Santo Sepulco (octagonal church), linked to the Knights Templar, sits proudly in the village and I imagine the cloaked knights walking along the paved streets. It's quiet except for the twittering of birds.

I'm relaxed but still keen to offload some weight from my pack. I talk to the Spaniard at the desk of the albergue, Hostal Rural San Andrés, who is helpful in my quest to send a package of things on to Santiago.[30] I manage to find about a kilo of stuff that I think I can do without and package it up.

Dinner is a pilgrim meal and great chatter with other pilgrims, including Edda and 'the Italians'. The couple they were travelling with are not with them anymore because they only planned to walk for a week.

The albergue fills up quickly so I'm grateful to have managed a bottom bunk again. A swarm of bike riders

---

29 Kit Kat and hot chocolate €1.70
30 Albergue €10; dinner €12; Coke €3; package sent to Santiago €12.90

arrive late in the day and take over the place with noise and bustle.

I struggle to sleep because the heating, as always, is too hot and no one likes to keep a window open in Spain.

> *Love is walking a deserted country path,*
> *followed by the call of the cuckoo.*

10 Wednesday 25 April: (ANZAC DAY) Torres del Rio to Logrono, 20kms

A room full of about thirty people with no open windows meant it was a sauna, so I had fractured sleep. The bikers were still fussing after nine last night and then up before six this morning. So much rustling and mucking around!

I decide to get up and leave even though it's only six-forty-five and dark. I figure I can have breakfast on the Way. It's about ten when I get to Viana and I'm so hungry! I wolf down egg, bacon, bread, then a chocolate bread plus tea.[31] The Camino passes through the old part of Viana and the medieval past is all around me. The old ramparts surround me as I leave the city through the medieval stone arch of *Portal San Felices*.

I FaceTime with the Kev – he's settled into a routine now. He has had the day off anyway for a public holiday.

There are poppies scattered everywhere so it's impossible not to remember ANZAC day. They are like beacons of red amongst the foliage around me.

---

31 Breakfast €7

I've now crossed over into the La Rioja region, famous for its wine.

I arrive in Logrono about two. I check into the big Albergue de Peregrinos de Logrono with lots of beds and have an average shower but it's good to stop.[32] I go looking for food in the old part of town and sit overlooking the gothic cathedral.

I think that I've timed this wrong because the kitchen is about to close and the pegerino meal is barely edible, but I need the fuel. An Asian man comes in, looking lost. He's obviously a pilgrim. I offer him a seat at my table, which he accepts.

He's from South Korea. He's trying to walk the Camino in two weeks because that's all the holiday time he has. I'm impressed by how good his English is and his sense of adventure, although I suspect that his adventurous spirit is more part naiveté.

I'm lucky to have a bottom bunk again and try to stay up as late as possible but I'm wriggling down into my sleeping bag before it's even dark.

> *Love is a poppy field to remind*
> *you of your grandfather.*

---

32 Albergue €7; average meal €11; apple + banana €1.50; hot chocolate (vending machine) €0.80

11

Thursday 26 April: Logrono to Ventosa, 18.4kms

I take my time getting up. My right achilles is sore, I need to take it easy. I start with coffee, fresh OJ and a croissant in a trendy bar that is full of business people. I stand out in my hiking gear.

I like my daily café con leche, the juice is always freshly squeezed, and the croissants are fresh, huge and buttery.[33] No need for butter or jam on them. It's also reasonably priced at three to four euros on average.

Most of the walk today is along a main highway, which isn't that pleasant. I'm sore and over it today so I stop for lunch at Navarrete.[34] I consider staying here due to my right achilles aching but it's much too early and I intended on getting to Ventosa, which is a detour on a scenic route off the main Camino. I dawdle for longer than intended.

I figure if I take it slow I'll be okay. The last hour is through farmland and I stop often and I'm happy to

---

33 Breakfast €3
34 Lunch €6

finally arrive around three-thirty and to be greeted with a drink of water!

This albergue, San Saturnino, is lovely and there is only room for eight pilgrims in my room. Oh my, a wonderful HOT HOT shower. I'm human again.

The Dane and Argentinian are here. I've seen them along the Way and am impressed that they are keeping pace with me even though I'm slow. They are easily twenty years older than me. I'm starstruck by her; I can't remember her name but she has the cutest white bob and she borrowed my toothpaste. Sigh. I want to be her when I'm in my 70s.

Despite there being a kitchen, it's not that convenient to cook for just one person and many of the pilgrims are travelling in groups so there's no one else to share food with. Besides, I'm lazy and tired. So off I toddle to a local bar and have a glass of red wine and fettuccine funghi – fabulous. What a treat to sit overlooking the vineyards as the spring sunshine fades and have food brought to me. I wish Kev were here to share it.[35]

After dinner, there's still a pocket of sunlight out the backyard and groups of pilgrims sit around tables, sharing meals they've cooked or hanging washing. The Italians are here so I sit with them to chat until the sun dips behind the buildings and it starts to cool down.

---

35 Albergue €11; dinner, including wine €7

There are a few Germans, an Englishman (Mike) and an American (Kevin) in my room. We talk about our respective walks and get to know each other. Mike and Kevin met at the start of the walk and have buddied up. Mike has done the Camino one-and-a-half times and wanted to come back to do it properly, plus he's between jobs as many walkers are. Reading between the lines, he's hoping to meet someone because the woman (back home) he likes is not available.

> *Love is wine and pasta for one,*
> *overlooking the vineyards.*

12 Friday 27 April: Ventosa to Azofra, 17.5kms

Last night I tried to read a novel that was left in the sitting room downstairs, mostly so I didn't have to justify going to bed at seven-thirty! The novel was boring so, after about forty minutes, I gave it up and snuggled into my sleeping bag. I love my orange and grey sleeping bag. I'm snug and safe inside it.

I sleep fitfully all night and am happy when it's late enough at six-thirty to get up. I'm having breakfast by about seven-fifteen after a quick FaceTime to Kev. No fires to put out there. Fresh juice, black coffee (language issue) and croissant are enough to get me going.[36]

I start well, covering about eleven kilometres by ten through wide country roads. I stop for a Cola Cao: my new favourite drink, which is just like chocolate Quick at home.[37] It goes down well. I take off my boots and socks to rest my feet. My right ankle is bothering me so I'm trying to take it easy.

---

36 €4
37 €1.80

As I'm walking I pass by what looks like a stone beehive. I sit inside it to rest a while and marvel at the architecture and mechanics of the building. It's in perfect condition – apart from being covered in graffiti inside. There are small triangular windows in all directions.[38]

I arrive at Azofra around one. The village has only about two hundred and fifty residents and is deserted. I check in and find that the rooms are like cubicles with two beds apiece at the Municipal de Peregrinos, which is luxurious compared to many other albergues.[39] After the obligatory long hot shower I wonder how I will fill the afternoon. There isn't much in the town and it takes about thirty minutes to walk up and down the main street. I buy some snacks and sunscreen and come back to the albergue to write in my journal and wash a few clothes.[40] I'm too tired to write much. An afternoon nap is in order and then I meet my roommate Eileen from the States.

As usual, there's a long wait for dinner because the Spaniards eat so late. I wander up to one of the local

---

38 I've had trouble finding out much information about these huts. They are called guardaviñas, which means vineyard guards. I'm guessing they were shelter for farmers.

39 Before I find the next albergue, I stop in a bar for lunch of tortilla and Coke €4; albergue is €10

40 Snacks €4; sunscreen €7.10; Cola Cao €1.80

bars and order a pilgrim meal.[41] One of the pilgrims comes in looking for a table so I offer her a seat at my table, which she is happy to accept. We have a funny time trying to communicate because she's French and knows zero English or Spanish and I know no Spanish and sparse French. There is more mime than words but we pass the time with lots of smiles. I speak in broken English now anyway.

After dinner I chat to Mike and Kevin, who are also staying at the same place. There are groups of people who I see from time to time who obviously meet up or walk together. It's easy to find sociable groups.

I fall into bed and sleep well.

Love is fresh orange juice.

---

41 €10

13 Saturday 28 April: Azofra to Granon, 21kms

I slept so well that I didn't hear Eileen come into the room last night. She was hanging out with the two German Walters who are in the room next door. I think I probably slept for about ten hours.

We are awake early. The Germans are always up early and packing their bags – not exactly quietly either. After the other day starting without any breakfast I resolved not to do this again, so I'm back at the Azofra bar where I had dinner last night.[42]

I have my usual pilgrim breakfast of fresh OJ, café con leche and a giant croissant. I bet the pilgrims didn't eat this well eight-hundred years ago. I like that the juice is always fresh and I actually like the coffee. My only issue is that I always need to find a tree within an hour for a wee. Other than at cafes and bars, I haven't seen a single public toilet so far.

I walk solidly for about three hours. There are cooler breezes today that make walking much more pleasant

---

[42] €4

after rain last night. I stop at Santo Domingo de Calzada for lunch and meet Margaret's friend Sally from the UK. We met on Facebook and have been chatting there while I've been on the Camino. Poor Sally has injured her knee and is stuck here while she recovers.

The town is buzzing, I'm guessing it's because it's a Saturday. We meet in one of the many squares and find somewhere for lunch. I eat calamari, which is yummy but greasy.[43]

I'm refreshed after the big break but queasy from the fried food. I motor along the path feeling like I'm flying. I aim to take a detour through the fields to Granon but I miss the turn somewhere, which means that I have to stay on the main road.

By the time I reach Granon around three-thirty, my euphoria is gone and I'm tired. I remind myself to pace myself.

I wonder where all the people are in these villages. Is it siesta time? You could hear a pin drop there are so few people around. I find the church, Iglesia san Juan Bautista, that I know other pilgrims are heading for. I check in and am given a mat on the floor. There's a friendly atmosphere here with a lot of love for each other. I'm wearing my bird beanie, which always gets a great reaction. One of the hospiteleros keeps grinning

---

43 €5

at me and hugging me (he's not creepy) and pointing at my hat.

There are about fifty pilgrims here already, over three levels of the church. Since there are only two or three bathrooms, I don't bother expecting a shower even though I'd love one. I figure a day without a shower won't hurt!

Sitting on my mat in the cold church isn't exactly appealing so I wander through the town of Granon. It's small so that's done in a short time, then I see a bar around the corner from the church. What else is there to do but sit in a bar with lots of other pilgrims?[44] I spend the afternoon in a bar drinking red wine with Mike (UK), Kevin (Ohio), Eileen (California), Walter (Germany), Mike (Germany), Walter (Germany) and Nora (Germany). One of these German Walters started the same day as me in SJPP; he turns eighty-two soon.

The wine is good and cheap at about two dollars Australian and I enjoy these people and their company but they appear to be on the pilgrimage for the socialness more so than I am. I go with the flow. At eight we head back to the church for a communal dinner of zucchini risotto, which is lovely but I'm still hungry afterwards.

---

44 Wine and various drinks €5

It's a unique experience to be in a room of fifty people from all over the world, sharing the work of cooking, then eating, then cleaning up.[45] The community spirit is alive. It gives me renewed hope for humanity, proof that we can all get on and work together.

At nine we head into a small area of the church for a pilgrim mass in three languages. A candle is passed around the circle and we are asked what we hope to gain from our pilgrimage. I can't speak when the candle comes to me because I'm too emotional. I'm still not sure what I'm hoping for despite being nearly two weeks in. And I'm curious about the fact that I lose my voice when it's my turn to speak.

Kevin and Mike are on mats across the room and Kevin is struggling with blisters. Eileen has a mat next to mine but she disappears somewhere and I don't see her before I go to sleep.

I am in my sleeping bag by about ten, fully clothed. The room is so cold that I doubt I'll get much sleep.

> *Love is a simple communal dinner*
> *amongst people of the world.*

---

[45] The church is a donativo, includes dinner and breakfast so I give €15

14 Sunday 29 April: Granon to Villambistia, 22kms

We wake early and scramble for the toilet and a quick coffee before heading out. This is the coldest morning since day one when it was close to freezing. I'm glad for gloves, hat and wet weather gear.

I'm now in the region of Castilla Y León, walking through peaceful villages. The weather has been changing all day. One moment the sun is out, the next, in come dark, black clouds that threaten rain. There are a lot of long stretches of pathways and I trudge along, feeling worn out.[46]

Those dark clouds hover and suddenly it starts to rain. I pull my rain jacket closer and the hat lower over my face and make sure the waterproof cover is over my pack. Here I am on the other side of the world in the middle of the Way and I ask myself: *Why?*

There's no one around me. I could get struck by lightning and it would take a while before someone found me. I try to calculate what time it is back home

---
46 The obligatory toilet stop and drink €4

but I can't focus. Then I calculate how far it is to my designated stop today. I've had enough.

It hails. I lower my head to try to protect my face. I start laughing. I laugh at the absurdity of what I'm doing. What am I trying to prove? Why am I doing this? Then I laugh at exactly that: the absurdity of what I'm doing and the fact that I'm doing it because I can. The hail stops as abruptly as it started and the sun explodes through the dark grey sky. I shake my head. This is just like Melbourne.

I cross a main road to a café and have a toilet stop and coffee. Mike and Kevin are there already. We nod to each other and they head out again.

I reach Tosantos but the albergue is full. It's gorgeously cosy inside and people are drinking at a bar. I'm homeless and left out. I'm probably thirty minutes too late for a bed and this is the first time that I haven't gotten one when I wanted it.

I reluctantly step back outside into the bitter cold to walk to the next town. This has got to be the longest two kilometres in my life. At last I find Albergue Villambistia in the tiny hamlet of Villambistia.[47] It's not as cosy as the last place but I don't care.

It's just me and a Spanish man in a room for twelve people. This feels awkward but I pick a bottom bunk on

---

47 Bed, dinner & breakfast €15

the other side of the room. I have a headache. I don't think I've eaten enough or had enough water today. I take some headache tablets and eat a banana, then head for the shower.

The shower is wonderfully hot. I stand in there so long that I expect someone to come pounding on the door to tell me to hurry up. I thaw out quickly. Within minutes I'm snuggled into my sleeping bag for a siesta.

I can't avoid the other person in the room. We chat from time to time and then go downstairs for a pilgrim meal at nine. Most of the pilgrim meals are nothing to be excited about but at least it's hot food and plenty of it. The Spaniard speaks good English. He is walking the Camino on his own to think about his life. He is married but not so happy. He says that the Camino is not giving him any answers so he might go home.

As I snuggle into my sleeping bag I contemplate the news that it might snow tomorrow!

Love is warmth and safety after a long, cold day.

15 Monday 30 April: Villambistia to Agés, 20.8kms

What a sleep! I'm generally not a good sleeper but there have been many nights on the Camino where I've slept well no matter what the bed is like. Despite feeling awkward about the other person in the room, I slept from nine until seven. I thought it would be cold but I was toasty and comfortable. So quiet and peaceful.

I am apprehensive about starting out with a forecast of 1°C and top of 8°C. But I put on a few layers plus a raincoat, hat, gloves and step out into the morning. The wind is brutal and my fingers are numb to begin with. But within half an hour I'm warm and I find the walk pleasant.

Thankfully the rain holds off all day (only a few drops) and I make sure I stop hourly and have a drink of water even though I don't feel like it. There are a few hills to start with and a long section of about twelve kilometres between towns but I'm enjoying the day.[48] I've decided that I walk better in the cold.

---

48 Toilet break; Cola Cao €1.80

At about three, I arrive in Agés. The approach to the town is beautiful with cows clanking their bells as they eat grass. I stop to take photos and some video of the cows. I start to think about how wonderful the sounds of the Camino are and decide that I'm going to record them from now on. I wish I'd thought of this two weeks ago.

The descent into the town is via an iridescent grassy hill with bright red poppies scattered here and there. It's a cute, bustling town.

El Pajar de Ages fills up not long after I check in. Then the rain comes. It's okay because I can have a hot shower in a real bathroom that is private and stay snug in my sleeping bag.

My room has two bunks and a single bed and I'm thankful for a bottom bunk. The other bunk has two young South Korean men who are hilarious with their stories of their Camino so far. They're ill-equipped for this walk. They don't have any provisions of note and keep leaving wallets and jackets behind. They have a baby blanket with the Simpsons on it that they take turns using.

In the single bed is the infamous Christina. She's German but lives in South America. I've heard her name mentioned a few times by Eileen and Mike but this is the first time I've met her. Christina is very sociable and laid back and between her, the Koreans and myself, the room is full of laughter.

In the bed above me is a German man who is proud to tell us that he walks forty kilometres per day. I wonder if he actually gets to enjoy it.

All up a good day. We walk over to another building for dinner. A pilgrim meal of soup, Paella, dessert and wine. Eileen is also there with the two Walters.[49]

Love is a cowbell.

---

[49] Café con leche €1.20; albergue with dinner and breakfast €20

16 Tuesday 1 May: Agés to Burgos, 22.5kms

It's not so cold this morning but cold enough. Most of the day is on public roads after about five kilometres of up and down.[50]

As I'm looking for the river route I spot a stork nest up high on a church. I'd seen these on YouTube and was looking forward to seeing them. They are magnificent.

Finally I get to the river on the approach to Burgos, which is a pleasant change. I decide to take the more scenic route to the city but I get lost. The river is lovely and walking along it is a relief after the public roads.

There are so many people out walking in family groups along the river and in the city because of the Labour Day holiday. This also means that shops are closed. Finally I find the lovely Divina Pastora, which is quiet and has great amenities. I'm sure I added another five kilometres to the day thanks to getting lost but I can rest now.

Divina Pastora is located above a chapel and is accessed by a small door that is hidden away. When

---

50 Toilet break; snack €4

I enter, it's by squeezing myself up a narrow spiral staircase with my bulky backpack to a room that sleeps sixteen people. It's a refuge from the bustle outside and I immediately relax as Sister Alice checks me in. There's free tea and coffee with a little sitting area and good hot showers.

I check in with Kev at home and he's stressing about running the business even though the cash flow is healthy. This brings me down and my knees ache. I have a long hot shower, which revives me, and then think about my dirty clothes. Thanks to Google I can find a laundry nearby. I bundle up my washing and head out into the city.

It's a long walk to the laundry but easier without all my gear. I sit quietly watching my clothes froth and twirl while rubbing my knees to revive them. Having clean clothes is such a luxury and it puts a smile back on my face.

It's lovely walking around the city, despite the sore knee. There's a real holiday feel to it and the late sunset means that the festive atmosphere goes until late. I take lots of photos of buildings, especially the ridiculously ornate Catedral de Santa Maria XIII. It's so ornate and over the top that I'm too disgusted by the opulence to go inside it.

I'm lonely wandering around on my own amongst so many tourists but I eventually choose an Italian looking place at the Plaza St Maria, and get some pasta.

The obligatory tasks: shower, washing, eating, have all worked to lift my spirits.[51]

Love is a hot shower.

---

51 Washing €6; albergue €6; dinner €15

17 Wednesday 2 May: Burgos to Hornillos del Camino, 21kms

I wake to someone singing in Spanish and playing the guitar. At first I'm not sure if it's a recording but I think it's real. It's just hard to tell at six am. I hear the word Camino in the first song, so I expect it is something to send us on our way. It's Sister Alice and she sings a second song but I understand none of it.

It's a great way to be woken but then we are told that we all have to be out by nine. I'm reluctant to leave this oasis. My feet hurt and now my left knee aches and for the first time I've woken with a headache. I think it's from the stuffiness of the room and lack of water. Dehydration is my biggest impediment.

But I figure that if I take it slow everything will warm up and my headache might go. As I'm walking out of Burgos, looking for somewhere to have breakfast, I see the Italians who I last saw in Abanos. We laugh and ask each other about our Camino. They have stayed in a large albergue right near where we're standing and tell me it's good.

We hug and say goodbye and I stop at a café close by. There are lots of backpacks, which is a sign of pilgrims. I put my pack amongst others and go inside to order my usual. As I'm coming out, there's Mike and Kevin with other pilgrims.[52] They also stayed at the nearby albergue and say it's fantastic. I sit with them feeling like I'm gatecrashing but they seem okay with it. It's good to chat with some familiar people.

Kevin is still struggling with his feet blistering so he and Mike are going to buy some new walking shoes at a sports outlet outside of the city. This means that they will be delayed walking for a while but Kevin can't get far each day and he's despondent about it.

After breakfast I'm better equipped for the day and leave the city after passing that decadent cathedral. I can say that this start to the day is the most intensely cold so far. It takes forever to get out of the city and there are not many places to rest. The path here feels much more open and so there is minimal protection from the icy wind. Apparently I have now entered the Meseta.[53]

My right knee is complaining, especially in the last half hour as I approach Hornillos del Camino, which is steep. The first two albergues are full. I see Christine

---
52 Breakfast €4.20

53 The flat plains of the Camino that last for about 220 kms, renowned for empty landscape and open sky

nab the last bed at the second. But this one, Meeting Point, has plenty of beds.[54] I'm happy to get bottom bunk again.

The facilities here are good. Hot drink, hot shower. Reset. I'm fatigued so it's good to stop. I'm missing home.

After a siesta, we all eat together on one long table. There are plenty of people to talk and share paella with. Dinner, being late as everywhere in Spain, means that I'm just about ready for bed straight afterwards.

There are two pilgrims in the bunk across from me, I can't remember their names but they've been walking together and were in the same room with Edda and me at Casa Mágica. I don't think they're a couple but I get the feeling that their relationship is complicated. I think he's German but I'm not sure about her. He complains a lot and said he's been having stomach troubles.

The room is suffocating with no windows but being in my sleeping bag is comforting and I snuggle up to listen to an audiobook despite it feeling antisocial.

Love is the universal language of music.

---

54 Albergue €10; dinner €10; snacks & drinks through the day €11.30

18 Thursday 3 May: Hornillos del Camino to Castrojeriz, 20.1kms

I sleep okay but the room is so hot with ten bodies in it. There is only white bread for breakfast so I opt for a quick coffee before heading out around seven-thirty. It's cool again this morning but not as biting as yesterday.

It's two-and-a-half hours before I can find another bar for breakfast.[55] I'm feeling faint with hunger and the road is open with no trees to shield me from the wind. I'm in the town of Hontanas where they have a gorgeous tiny chapel of Santa Brigida. I could sit here for hours in this tiny chamber with Brigida. She's a cool chick, having made her own pilgrimage of three years back in the 1300s with her husband, later being canonised by a Pope.

But hunger spurs me on.

After Hontanas the path is relatively flat for the rest of my way. I love the birds that perch on shrubs and twitter away. It feels like they are my walking companions. I've tried to take photos but they are too quick for me. The countryside here is open and flat.

---

55 €4

Just about every hour I need to pee, which is not easy with no tree coverage and NO public toilets. I still haven't seen a public toilet in Spain. There are times when I have to quickly squat in a ditch and hope no one comes along the path.

I approach Castrojeriz around twelve-thirty and I'm ready to stop. I get a coffee at the first bar I see (to warm up and pee).[56] It's so good to get out of the wind. Across from the bar is the Church of Our Lady of the Apple. Like many of the churches it's opulent. I don't bother visiting it because I'm tired.

This town has only about five hundred occupants and must be in permanent siesta, it's so sleepy and deserted.

I find Casa Nostra, opposite the church of St Dominic (closed), which I had picked from the guidebook as a good place to stay.[57] Not bad for the price but it's cold. The shower is lukewarm so it's a quick shower from waist down (hand held shower head). Strangely enough it does warm me up but I need to get into my sleeping bag to try to defrost, fully clothed.

And guess who comes into my room? The Italians. Their gear is already on their beds but they have been out looking for food. They are sweet and offer to share

---

56 Coffees during the day €2.40

57 Albergue €4

a meal of pasta with me. How can I refuse? They are looking after me because I am *solo*.

The Italians live near Florence. I finally learn their names: Maurizio and Virginia. They have limited English but we manage. The kitchen is not well equipped and freezing but this has to be one of the best meals I've ever had. Warming and fresh and homemade. It's just tuna, pasta and tomato but I cannot explain how good it is. They make a show of setting the table with what they can find, including using tissues as napkins. The table has an old red and white plastic checkered cover over it, which gives the kitchen a rustic Italian persona. We laugh about men cooking because Maurizio says he never cooks at home.[58]

It's so cold that I go to bed early, fully dressed including beanie. I'm lucky enough to have a single bed while most of the other beds are bunks. I drift off to sleep to the sound of Virginia playing her bubble game on her phone.

Love is the generosity of strangers.

---

58 I buy lemon yogurt to share for dessert €2 (big spender!)

19 Friday 4 May: Castrojeriz to Boadilla, 19.1km

It's a long, cold night with no heating and the Finnish man on the top bunk across from me snores so loudly the walls vibrate. In the middle of the night I heard Maurice get up and shake him to stop the snoring, but it lasted only a few minutes.

I'm out the door around seven-twenty and don't bother to stop anywhere for breakfast. It's intensely cold and the first thing I see as I leave the town is a squiggly path going up the mountain. The day is just waking, the clouds dark and foreboding. Tackling the hill is actually good because it warms me even though I can't feel my face anymore. The problem starts when I have to go down the other side. My left knee is in pain.[59]

By lunchtime I have had enough of the mean wind that pushes me side to side, so I decide that I won't go to Fromista as planned. The stretch between Itero and Boadilla (about ten kilometres) is open, long and lonely. The Italians pass me at some stage when I'm resting

---

59 I stop for breakfast €4

and take a photo of me 'for you husband'. Just imagine his italian accent.

Farther on, I pass them again as Maurizio stands guard with his coat screening his wife while she pees. There's nowhere to hide. No trees or long grass or even a ditch.

Finally, I stop at En El Camino, an albergue in Boadilla, which is bustling and cosy.[60] It's impossible to connect to WIFI, and there's no signal even with my SIM card and that makes me more despondent because I can't talk to Kev.

There are plenty of people I know here, as in Camino know, like the two German Walters, Mike and Kevin and Eileen. It's Walter's eighty-second birthday today.

I have a shower, which is wonderfully hot *hot* HOT! I do not want to get out of it. It's so good, especially with washed hair (smelling like honey). Human again. Then I snuggle up in my sleeping bag to thaw out and have a snooze.

Dinner is lentil soup followed by beef stew. My childhood has collided with the Camino because the lentil soup is delicious (even got some carrots) and the beef stew is just like goulash.[61] This meal, coupled with

---

[60] Albergue €10; dinner €8 (food fit for a queen); tomorrow's breakfast €3

[61] This is apparently a typical Castilian meal prepared by the owners of this albergue, the Begona family

red wine, is a sure way to thaw anyone out and dissolve any physical and mental pains.

I hear 'Happy Birthday' singing from another room and smile at the thought of Walter being surrounded by so much Camino love. He walks to remember his wife and must feel the loss.

After dinner I snuggle into my sleeping bag to listen to Brené Brown on an audio book. The Italians have also stopped here and are sleeping near other Italians in a mezzanine above me. None of them are good at whispering quietly, which makes me giggle. I'm drifting into sleep by nine-thirty.

Love is nourishing food.

20 Saturday 5 May: Boadilla to Carrion de Los Condes, 26km

What a difference today! It's still cool but bright blue skies and twittering birds all around me. I'm aiming for Carrion de Los Condes and I know it's going to be a big day to make up for yesterday's early stop even though it was close to my average daily kilometres. I'm determined to pace myself by stopping every hour. The whole day is virtually flat and I decide on a detour from the main Camino that only adds another kilometre (according to my John Brierley guidebook).

Just before the river turn, I bump into Kevin and Mike, who are bouncing along the Way. Kevin is still struggling with his footwear. They push off ahead of me and I watch them disappear into the distance. They have also opted for the detour.

After Fromista via Villovieco, the path leaves the town via farm tracks. It's along the river for about ten kilometres so of course I'm in my happy place.

This is one of the best days so far. There is hardly anyone walking this route and it's a grassy pathway that's sheltered from the cold wind. It's a joy to follow the water and be surrounded by trees and farmland.

For a break I stop at a picnic table to have something to eat. The grass is waist high and the wind is whooshing around me and the birds are twittering. I peel a mandarin that is delicious. In this moment I'm so happy. I ponder the dreamlike aspect of sitting here on my own, with my backpack, in the middle of the Spanish countryside, snacking on a mandarin and a bag of nuts. The sun is warm on my face and neck and I could not feel any more at peace or lucky.

I continue to follow the waterway. I have a feeling it isn't actually a real river but some kind of aqueduct to service the farms. There isn't much water in it but it's enough to give me the river vibe. At a paddock a donkey comes up to me to say hello and walks with me for a while, chewing grass casually. I stop often to sit by the river on the grass and listen to the wind. I pass Kevin a few times looking pained with his shoes off.[62]

I arrive at Carrion around three. I try a couple of albergues only to find them full. After wandering around I find Monastery Espiritu Santo. I'm hot and bothered and happy to get a single bed in a dorm room. As usual there's a welcome hot shower to make me feel good again.

At six-thirty I walk around the town, have a coffee in a square, then go to a church nearby where a man is

---

[62] I stop for lunch at a café with Mike & Kevin and another young American who I don't know €6.40

playing flamenco guitar. I enjoy listening but I don't stay too long because I'm getting cold. On the way back to my room I pass Kevin and Mike in the hallway. I wonder if they think I'm stalking them.

I share a meal of pasta with Bee from England. We pool resources and hustle for space in the communal kitchen. We eat pasta, a big punnet of strawberries then some chocolate and retire to our beds early.[63]

Love is a ripe mandarin.

---

[63] Albergue €5 (it's actually a donativo but they 'tell' us how much to 'donate'); coffee €1.40; dinner €1

21 Sunday 6 May: Carrion des Los Condes to Ledigos, 23.4km

The sleep in the Espiritu Santo convent is great. Single beds for a change. Bee is in a bed next to me and the room is almost full. I'm up again around six-forty, breakfast at seven (the usual), walking by seven-thirty.[64]

Today is flat and boring. Hours of nothing, not even a rock to sit on. I try to imagine the Roman roads that once ran through this area. History weaves around and through me. There's an especially long section of over ten kilometres with no town in between. Luckily there is a pop-up café about four kilometres in and I sit with Kevin and Mike for a snack.[65]

Somehow we keep bumping into each other. Kevin can't walk as fast as he'd like because of his feet. He's frustrated by it and thinks he's holding Mike back but I can tell that Mike is more than happy to go with the flow, Camino-style.

I arrive in Ledigos and the albergue El Palomar, around two-forty-five and FaceTime Kev as soon as I

---

64 Breakfast €2.50
65 Sausage sandwich at food truck €5; Coke €1.40; coffee €1.20

check in. Because it's been hot and sunny all day, it's perfect weather to wash clothes. It's warm and sunny until late (it's around seven-thirty now and I just moved to sit in the shade). I plan on a short walk tomorrow because my feet are weary and I've done more than my planned twenty for the past two days.

This town is tiny. The only thing worth seeing is a tiny church at the top of the hill. There is a restaurant where I'm staying but I like the vibe of the bar on the west of the town because it's bathed in the evening sun. I enjoy pasta and wine and listen to other patrons chattering around me.[66]

Love is long sunny days.

---
66 Albergue €7; dinner €13

22 Monday 7 May: Ledigos to Sahagun, 16.4kms

I sleep well because the room isn't heated, although I stirred more often than usual. I'm slow getting up so it's almost eight by the time I have breakfast and am on the Way, the latest start so far. It's already heating up.

I'm weary so I plan to stop in Sahagun. It's not far but if I go further, it will have to be another ten kilometres and I don't think I can handle that today. Even knowing that this will be a shorter day and it's relatively flat, the walking is tedious.

These long, flat paths mean that there isn't as much to worry about in terms of walking. But it does mean that there's plenty of time to think. Lots of thinking time can be bad because all of these conversations swirl around in my head. It makes me realise just how much I talk to myself.

A lot of the talk isn't kind. Sometimes I'm dredging up the past or berating myself for the way I handled something. After a while I get angry with myself for this self-talk so then I start telling myself off for thinking these thoughts. I try to change the subject, think of more positive things or distract myself by listening to the birds.

I'm realising why people avoid this part of the Camino. It can make you crazy. There are lots of people in groups who talk to each other or wear headphones to listen to music. I resist both. I came here for a reason. I just don't know what it is.

I walk over an old bridge, then the grand gateway into Sahagun. It's old and atmospheric as I enter an old part of the city and look for the Monastery de Santa Cruz. It is literally ON the Camino. I love how you can be trudging along and there is the place you've been looking for, the door literally within arm's reach.

What an oasis! I'm hot and bothered when I arrive and the man on the desk gives me a drink of cold water. The room has two bunks (I get bottom) and so far no one else is here. There's also a bathroom with toilet and shower just for this room. What luxury!

I enjoy spending time here by myself, have a long shower and shave my legs and put my silk skirt on without feeling self-conscious.

There's a supermarket close by. I wander over. I guess I've done well for three weeks without having to buy any supplies. Food is cheap so I stock up for the shared meal later tonight. Everyone is expected to bring something. I buy myself some afternoon tea and enjoy it in the afternoon sun in the courtyard of the monastery.

At four-thirty we have pilgrim welcome tea where we sit and get to know each other. There are always plenty of people to talk to from all over the world and I'm amazed by how many people are walking the Camino again and again.

A special pilgrim mass is at six-thirty. We're blessed and able to take a pilgrim blessing, written in our own language, away with us. Wanda and Gary are here. I met them a day or so ago in a café. They are well versed in the religious ceremony. I'm guessing they are catholic.

At eight I go to the dining room. There are about twenty people here, each person contributing something to a shared meal. A wonderful meal of soup followed by pasta and of course plenty of wine.[67]

I enjoy snuggling down into my sleeping bag in my bottom bunk without anyone else in the room. I figure since it's almost nine-thirty I doubt anyone else will turn up.

A small blister is forming on my right heel so I'll keep an eye on that. I'm lucky that I have managed to walk so far without blisters.

Love is the luxury of a single room.

---

[67] Donativo €5 (another 'donativo' where they tell us what to 'donate'); Cola Cao €1.80; supermarket €8.66

23 Tuesday 8 May: Sahagun to El Burgo Ranero, 17.4km

Not long after I snuggled down to sleep last night, two young women came bounding into the room. They're cycling the Camino and bike riders get last preference but I also think they just keep cycling until they lose daylight. It meant my peace was shattered but it wasn't too bad. I had lots of time in the afternoon to enjoy the quiet.

I'm ready by seven-thirty – just as well because it warms up quickly. I bump into Mike and Kevin just as I step out into the street. We walk together for a while, then I hold back to allow them to get ahead of me. As much as it's great to chat, I love being on my own and I'm worried they might think I'm stalking them.

The first ten kilometres is effortless, then the flat open road becomes monotonous and boring and the monkey brain starts taking over.

Today I'm nursing the first signs of blisters. I don't want them to become a problem. I wear my sandals for the last hour just to be sure. This cools me down as well.

As I approach the town of El Burgo Renaro, I spot Mike and Kevin again. They're having lunch with another couple. I stop for a drink. Kevin is happy. He's been walking in Mike's sandals instead of runners and they make all the difference to him. He has renewed energy and enthusiasm without pain in his feet. He's keen to push on so that he can buy a pair of his own sandals in Leon.

We talk about Cruz de Ferro, which is about a week away by my estimation. Kevin has two small stones to leave there for his children. He plans to pray that they always know Jesus because he worries about how their lives will be if they don't.

I have my small heart rock from Tralfamadore but I don't tell anyone about my plans.[68] In fact, most of the time on the Camino I listen to what others talk about but rarely tell them my thoughts. I'm not sure why this is.

I plan to stay here for the night because the weather looks like it'll turn nasty. Mike and Kevin are keen to push on. As I watch their retreating backs, I'm aware that my two Camino brothers are leaving and that I may not see them again. I get a pang of remorse and wonder if I should push on too but I know that physically I won't keep up and that would go against my Camino

---

68 Tralfamadore is my childhood home

plan. After they're gone I regret that I didn't get their contact details.[69]

The albergues fill fast. I'd hate to be here during summer because I don't think it would be easy to get a bed. I try one that does have a bed but the host is rude and the place has a negative atmosphere about it. The next albergue, Domenico Laffi, is a donativo and I instantly want to stay. It's an adobe-style building made from mud and straw and is packed to the brim with people. I don't think they can fit another bed in the place.

I check in with Kev on FT – the Internet is good here. I wash my socks and spot the French lady from Agés and we smile at each other.

After a shower I look out to see the storm has brewed and it's spitting as I head to La Bostra del Abode, one of the restaurants across town (only a street away). I'm so hungry and this place is cosy and friendly. I choose a purely vegetarian meal: chickpeas with potatoes plus a salad as well as grilled asparagus. I have to take a photo of it, it's so good. This must be about the best meal I've had, even though I've had some great ones. As I'm eating, the showers erupt from the black clouds; I hope that Kevin and Mike have gotten to shelter.

---

69 Unfortunately I don't see them again

When the deluge abates, I walk around town and take photos of the storks up on top of the church. I love the clicking sound they make in their nests. The rain has eased but winds are still high. My socks might dry quickly!

Back at the albergue I sit in the common room amongst the pilgrims. There's no room anywhere else. There are people with guitars so there are a few sing-alongs and lots of laughter.[70]

They can fit more pilgrims in because they don't turn people away. There are now people camped out on the floor and along the window seats.

In a couple of days I'll be in Leon. I'm looking forward to stopping for a day and have booked a room for two nights.

Love is a stork in its nest.

---

70 I donate €1 to light a red candle in a tiny chapel and say a prayer for all the wonderful people in my life; drinks & snacks €12.50; albergue (donativo) €3; dinner €10.50; Piso Alcazar de Toledo hotel €80

24. Wednesday 9 May: El Burgo Ranero to Mansilla de las Mulas, 19.3kms

It's just getting light as I leave El Burgo Ranero to the sound of the storks clicking to each other from their nest atop of the church in the centre of town. The rain has passed on thankfully. My sleep wasn't so great with everyone packed tight into the albergue (and hot as usual) but the community spirit was high.

Today's walk is one long path of gravelly surfaces alongside a road. I'm weary and not enjoying the landscape. It's flat, flat, flat. It means I don't have to worry too much about the terrain and that means I'm thinking about things again. My monkey brain is louder.

Another pilgrim passes me with long loping strides. He smiles, says 'Buen Camino' and asks if I'm feeling good. I smile back but I'm not feeling it. He disappears into the darkness and the last thing I see is the guitar strapped to his back. It makes me feel old.

The first stop is at about thirteen kilometres and I can't believe how quickly it goes. Time does move quickly on the Camino.

I wish I hadn't opted to start without breakfast, though, because three hours of walking takes me over the hunger threshold. Croissant, cafe con leche plus fresh juice are the order, of course.[71] By the time I get to Mansilla I'm tired and have a headache. Most probably dehydrated, again.

The blisters on my heels are growing. I'm surprised that I'm getting any after over three weeks of walking. I expected them earlier than this. They aren't too bad compared to some I've seen that make me squeamish.

As I'm checking into the albergue there's someone getting first aid on their feet. I don't look to closely.

After a hot shower, banana and some headache tablets, I'm recalibrated. This leaves me with plenty of time to wander around and get supplies. I explore the walled city and buy yogurt and ingredients to make pasta. The rio Esla runs alongside one of the walls and past a beech forest that is mysterious and medieval. I watch someone washing their dogs in the river. If it were warmer I'd take a swim myself.

The albergue, a municipal, is community-minded and the kitchen is pumping from about four until eight. I manage to squeeze in to make some pasta and then watch everyone around me.[72]

---

71 Breakfast €4
72 Albergue €5; supermarket €5

The South Koreans cook a feast of white rice, greens etc. A group of Italians spend three hours making tagliatelle from scratch, then singing and dancing loudly. Luckily the rule is that lights go out at ten in these albergues, otherwise we'd get no sleep. The rooms are jam-packed and too warm and the bed isn't that comfortable but at least I have the bottom bunk.

Love is being surrounded by people of the world.

25 Thursday 10 May: Mansilla de las Mulas to Leon, 18.1km

I've been looking forward to Leon because I've planned a rest day. I'm fatigued and need a rest from people. I'm looking forward to a room to myself after three weeks of sharing.

After a quick breakfast in the village (where the barman stirs me for not ordering in Spanish) I head out of the village by crossing rio Esla towards Leon.[73] The long shadows of the sun rising behind me never get boring.

It's already eight by the time I'm on the Way but today I'm not in a hurry. I've booked a hotel room away from the crowds for two nights and I'm hoping there's a bath as promised on the booking.com page. It's a cheap room but it has to be at least something better than a jammed-in bunk bed where I'm inches away from a stranger.

An American man is walking with his teenage son and two of the son's friends. He walks with me for about thirty minutes as the teens walk farther ahead.

---

73 Breakfast €4

I'm learning that on the Camino this isn't unusual and I'm not threatened by it. People are simply keen to chat with everyone without ulterior motive.

I'm happy when we part – they stop for breakfast – because I prefer to walk on my own, but I hope that I was friendly and not standoffish. Then I wonder why I'm worrying when I most likely won't see them again.

The guidebook says that this section of the Camino is laborious because there's lots of walking along the highway and through industrial areas. It's tough but not as bad as I expected and I'm glad that I didn't catch a bus, as the book suggested (although I was tempted).

I approach the outskirts of Leon at about twelve but it takes forever to get to the centre where my hotel is. That's okay because I can't check in until one anyway, another reason to take my time.

It takes a while to find my hotel. Turns out the hotel isn't a hotel, but an apartment that a women rents rooms from. No one is here when I arrive at one-thirty. I ring the bell and phone several times with no answer.

I ask next door (a swanky clothing store) if they speak English. They're friendly and try to help but can't work out what I want so I lug my backpack out for some lunch. I'm feeling out of kilter being off the Camino even if it's only a few blocks. The safety net is gone. I'm wishing I'd just gone to an albergue and booked a private room instead.

When I return there's someone to answer the intercom but they don't have my booking even though I made it two nights ago on booking.com. Luckily she has a room for me anyway.

It's great to be able to spread my stuff out and relax in my own space. I have a queen bed and a desk. Despite the pillows being fat I know that I'll enjoy hanging out here for two nights.

Thanks to Google, I can find a laundry in the next street and I take my stinky washing there.

After siesta time I wander around the city. Everything is close and I find the Camino easily and watch pilgrims wandering around. The cathedral is huge and I make a mental note to look inside tomorrow.

I find a restaurant with an outdoor area that faces the setting sun and overlooks Basilica de San Isidoro. I eat dinner late (they don't start until eight) in an outside restaurant facing the sun. Paella of course, with wine. I enjoy the luxury of having food made for me as I have most nights so far.[74] It allows me to people watch and to listen to other people's conversations.

An American is talking to another pilgrim at the next table. We pilgrims can spot each other without our gear. He tells his companion that he walks the Camino once a year to lose weight and that the rest of

---

74 Lunch of potato tortilla €5; laundromat €6; dinner with wine €19

the year he doesn't worry about it. His aim is to lose ten kilograms.

It's still light when I get back to my room but I go to bed early.

Love is a room of your own.

26 Friday 11 May: Leon, rest day

I slept fitfully (pillow too fat) but it's good to lie around and not rush off. This is the first time since I left home. I did find a bath (shared bathroom) but of course there's no plug. I assume it's to deter people from using it. But, I'm desperate to have one so I use my water bottle lid to plug it up. Lovely and hot!

I take my time to venture out into the city. I need to sort my SIM card because it runs out tomorrow. It's already eleven, and I wait almost an hour at Vodafone but now I have another SIM to last until I go home.[75] At least the girl here is much friendlier than the one I got in Madrid.

While I'm waiting, Sara tries to call me on Facebook Messenger but I can't take it.[76] I call her back once I have the SIM sorted out. We chat about things and it feels like she might be in the same city as me.

I'm reminded of how different it is to travel now, compared to the days when Kev and I backpacked in

---

75 SIM €20 for 28 days
76 My beautiful sister

1990 before mobile phones and internet. How did we survive?

I also get some Compeed patches for my blisters. They are the cure that everyone on the Camino talks about. The blisters are only small but I don't want them to get debilitating.

It's about twelve by the time I get to think about food. I'm so hungry that I opt for chocolate con churros and coffee! So good! I sit at a bar listening to people all around me from all over the world.[77]

It's cold today and maybe because I'm not walking I'm feeling it. I go back to my room for warmer clothes. While I'm back at my room I have a big chat to Kev on FaceTime, and then go back out. By then the streets are empty. After more than three weeks I still can't get used to siesta time! This means that shops have all closed and there's not much to see or do until later, so I go back to mooch around my room, looking at all the gorgeous Spanish shoes in the shop windows on the way.

I'm feeling hungry and in need of some seriously healthy food after eating out so much. There's a supermarket close by so I stock up. I buy salad, yogurt and muesli. I have a punnet of strawberries and a kilo

---

77 Breakfast €4.20. I would never eat like this at home!

of bananas. When I get it all back to my room it dawns on me that I'll have to carry a lot of this tomorrow so I aim to eat as much as I can.

Problem is that the punnets of strawberries here are a kilo, not two-fifty grams like back home. I wonder if eating a kilo of strawberries will upset my stomach.

After siesta when everything is open again I take the plunge and pay money to visit the cathedral in the centre of the city. It's impressive from the outside and equally impressive on the inside, although dark.

I walk around with headphones to guide me through the cathedral. There are lots of details about the reasoning behind different windows. These windows are massively high and beautiful stained glass masterpieces. Hearing about the story behind them is interesting (even though I forget most of it immediately) but the whole tour only lasts about ten minutes and then I'm out the door again.

I wander around aimlessly. It's not right to be off the Camino and I'm missing the routine of it and talking to other pilgrims. Here I'm just one out of thousands of people walking the streets.

As I turn a corner near the cathedral I spot Eileen (US) and Michael (Germany). My suspicions of them hooking up might be right but without asking them outright I'll probably never know. Eileen had told me snippets about a long and difficult marriage back in the States, so I'd say she would be hesitant to start anything.

I say hi and we all sit at a table overlooking the cathedral and order tapas. For around two Aussie dollars this is so cheap: red wine with food. They keep paying for mine.

We have two rounds and chitchat, then Frank (I think he's from Germany) turns up. There's always someone to bump into on the Camino. We get the waiter to take a group photo and email each other our contact details.

Michael is attentive to Eileen and I don't think that I'm that bad at reading signals but I can feel that she is trying to hold him at bay. They talk about finding somewhere to eat dinner, and ask me to join them, but I have to eat some more of my supermarket food to reduce the weight so I wave goodbye and go back to my room. It's already about eight-thirty by then anyway.[78]

Love is a kilo of strawberries to yourself.

---

78 Supermarket €13; Compeed €6.70; Cathedral entry €6

27 Saturday 12 May: Leon to Villar de Mazarife, 21.8kms

I'm happy to get my boots on again – they're so comfy – and get out of the city. The wind is extremely cold out there today despite the bright blue sky. The way out of Leon is a lot of slog. Maybe I'm out of rhythm after a day off, so I decide to take a 'scenic' route after passing a sign with an option to turn at three different roads.

I'm happy with this decision straight away because wide country roads open up before me with purple wildflowers everywhere. The wind is still sharp on my cheeks but the open fields are flat for most of the way.

I stop for a break in a café that is wonderfully warm and order a hot chocolate. The room is full of pilgrims and locals chatting and it's welcoming. I could stay here all day but I push on.

About thirty minutes before my next break, my feet are hot and aching. I take my boots off and wear my sandals with my merino socks. This helps but I'm now ready to stop. By the time I reach Villar de Mazarife I'm chilled right through. My pack is extra heavy thanks to all the food I bought Thursday!

I'm tired and grumpy but can't decide where to stay. I pass one place, then two, for some reason deciding that neither is good. I finally pick the third albergue, Tio Pepe.

I check in and go upstairs to the room. It has only two bunks in it but that's all there's space for. The packs hardly fit in and for any of us to come in and out of the room we almost have to go out into the corridor and rotate. I'm disappointed that I didn't stop at one of the other places and negative thoughts cram my head. To top it off there's only a top bunk left but I guess so far I've been lucky, mostly getting bottom bunks.

Since there is no room to move and there are three other women in the room, I opt to walk around the village with the obligatory storks nesting on the church towers and a tractor rumbling down the main street. Not much to see because of course it's siesta time.

In an attempt to warm up I sit in the sun in the courtyard. I have a picnic from my supermarket stash: cheese, salami, biscuits etc. This improves my mood.

I can't be bothered having a shower, because there's a queue (two showers for 26 or so people) and it's too cold to undress. So I snuggle up into my sleeping bag for a snooze. I can't even look at my phone because there's no signal on it. I'm happy in the sleeping bag and begin to thaw out. I figure it's only one night and I couldn't have walked any further today.

At seven, I go downstairs for the pilgrim meal. It has a cozy atmosphere in the bar and the good thing is that pilgrims will sit with you, which is comforting. I don't have high expectations for this meal because so far everything else has been disappointing. Even the price for my bed is steep for what I get.

All my complaints evaporate once the food arrives: veggie soup (divine), then chicken drumsticks with chips followed by crème caramel. All with red wine. Followed up with a shot of grappa! You cannot underestimate how a good hot meal can bring you back into a positive mindset and make everything good in the world again.[79]

Back in the room it's hot even though there's no heating. Soon all three women are snoring. Probably four by the time I go to sleep.

C'est la vie.

Love is hot food when you're frozen.

---

[79] Drinks €4.90 (I see this as the cost of using a toilet); albergue €9; dinner €12

28 Sunday 13 May: Villar de Mazarife to San Justo de la Vega, 24.9km

This spring weather is changeable. It's another brisk day but the wind is not as combative as yesterday and the sky is bright blue. My body and feet feel good today.

I've enjoyed lovely country roads again, with more storks in strange places. Around midday I arrive at the gorgeous medieval town of Hospital de Orbigo as bells are chiming the hour and churchgoers dressed in black spill out of a church (stork nest balancing on the tower) into the narrow street.

As I turn the corner I can see the Puente de Orbigo, a medieval bridge that dates back to the thirteenth century and is built over a Roman bridge. This is a spectacular landmark.

I visualise hundreds of years of foot passengers this bridge has had: fights between Christians and Moors, traders from the Roman times or Visigoths slaughtering Swabians, not to mention countless pilgrims making their way to Santiago.

I cross the bridge and look down over rio de Orbigo and marvel how well the bridge is restored.

I walk through farmland, past more villages and up over hills past Las Casa de los Dioses Cantina where a local called David gives out free gifts. I don't stop to talk to him because other pilgrims are already there and I'm keen to sit amongst the trees to contemplate the hills.

Some of these roads aren't marked as well as others and I'm fearful of getting lost because it's getting late in the day. I need to remember that the Camino provides, as it has done for twenty-seven days. I find my way easily.

It's about four-thirty by the time I find the albergue, which makes me wonder again about the distance. It was one thirty when I got to the albergue yesterday and it was only about three kilometres less. I have tried to pace myself well but the day was harder than what I expect for twenty-five kilometres. I'm sure the distances in the guidebook are more fluid than concrete.

The albergue, Hostal Juli, doesn't look like much from the outside and it's intimidating coming through the bar filled with old Spanish men. But, yes, they have a bed. I'm happy because even though Astroga is only about an hour away I am ready to stop. My feet are now screaming at me after walking up over the rolling hills.

I'm led through the car park to the dorm room (past an intimidating German Shepherd). Imagine my surprise when I find no one else is in the albergue yet!

I have a long, wonderfully hot shower and put clean underwear on – the simple pleasures – then sort through my stuff and get better organised. I've lost count of how many times I've emptied and repacked my pack.

I wonder if anyone else will be staying here for the night. I pick a bottom bunk in one corner. The door can't be locked and I wouldn't do that anyway in case someone else came to stay but it feels remote out here.

There's a sensor light at the front so I figure that I'll know if someone comes. I put my heavy aluminum drink bottle close by in case I need to use it as a weapon.

I go over to the bar to see what they might offer for dinner. They do have a pilgrim meal but not until eight when the cook comes in. I wait in the bar and drink a coffee to kill time and write in my journal with Spanish TV in the background.

As dinnertime approaches, two people enter the room from a side door. It's Wanda and Gary from Queensland. We chat and giggle about how we keep bumping into each other. Wanda is very sick with a chest cold and I wonder if I should sit next to her but it would be rude not to. We eat the pilgrim meal together. It's not great food but bolsters me.[80] Wanda and Gary leave through

---

80 Drinks €4.30; albergue €6; dinner €9.50

the side door to their private room upstairs while I go out the back door past the German Shepherd and cross the car park to the dormitory. There are still no other pilgrims checked in.

Love is clean underwear.

29 Monday 14 May: San Justo de la Vega to Rabanal, 24.2km

Oh wow! It ends up that NO ONE else checked in to the albergue, which means that I had the whole place to myself. What bliss. I did feel worried lying there on my own, thinking that someone may come in and murder me and no one would know. But I was so snug in my bunk and there was nobody else but me snoring. I'd say that I had at least ten hours of sleep.

It's around eight by the time I head out because I check in with Kev and then Les.[81] I decide to have breakfast in Astorga because it's only about an hour away.[82]

I arrive in the main square just in time to see the famous mechanical figures clang the bell on the hour, then I have a cooked breakfast of bacon and eggs. Not a bad way to start the day.

The day is chilly (not as much as yesterday) and changeable and I take my time looking around Astorga. There's the Episcopal Palace, a Gaudi building, and

---

81 Les is a friend and colleague
82 Big cooked breakfast of eggs, bacon & coffee €7.50

lovely churches everywhere, along with lots of quaint streets and buildings.[83] It's a clean town and probably a great place to stay but I push on.

I decide that Rabanal is a good place to aim for since I'm feeling strong. It's a fair distance and more than I want to go in a day but I figure I'll see how I go, especially since I started late and took time having breakfast. The long flat stretches of the Way are now gone since I've left the Meseta. There's a definite incline and I can see snow-capped mountains ahead with those wind turbines that I love.

Those cheeky cuckoo birds still follow me everywhere and I pledge to record the sound sometime on this walk. I haven't managed it yet despite almost four weeks of trying. Every time I get my camera or phone out, they stop their cuckoos.

Not far out from Rabanal, I pass over Puente de Pañote – a quaint bridge over rio Rabanal de Viejo – then on up towards mixed woodland, past the ghost of the 300-year-old pilgrim oak that was felled in a recent storm.

To my right is a rickety fence line that has makeshift crosses (made from a variety of sticks, string, plastic) woven into it by droves of passing pilgrims. It goes on for ages. I think about adding a cross of my own

---

83 Gaudi is a Spanish architect from late 1800s, notable for his gothic style buildings

but decide that I'm being hypercritical following along with something for the sake of it when I'm not actually religious.

It takes me longer than I expect and I'm feeling tired when I reach Refugio Gaucemo – a donativo – at four-thirty. All day I had a good feeling about this place; I'm not disappointed.

The town is beautiful, just with one street and cats lounging around everywhere. I made it just in time for afternoon tea. And I mean real tea with milk and sugar and good old English biscuits for dunking. It feels civilized to sit in the garden near the barn with a group of pilgrims in the waning afternoon sun with a teacup in hand.

It's not especially warm in the barn but at least I have a bottom bunk. It's dark too so not a great place to hang out. I wander around the village – which doesn't take long – and think about food for dinner. There are a few places to eat but I don't want to spend money on a big meal. The kitchen is well-equipped so I go in search of food. I find a tiny shop around the corner and buy pasta, avocado and Parmesan cheese.[84]

After some pasta, it's time for vespers at seven. Since it's all in Spanish, it's lost on me and it's cold in the tiny chapel. There's meant to be an order of monks who

---

84 Lit a candle in a chapel €1; algergue (donativo) €8; food €4.50

fill the church and chant Gregorian chants but they're nowhere to be found.

I sneak out as soon as I can and go back to sit in the common room where everyone huddles around a fire. I read a few books that are lying around but feel too restless to stay for long, or to talk to people much.

I realised as I was walking today that tomorrow is what I have been waiting for: to leave my heart at Cruz de Ferro. I have the stone in my pack. It's travelled the world a few times now and is a small piece of a special place, so tomorrow it's a hike up to 1515m.

I think about Mike and Kevin. They will have been through here days ago. I wonder if Kevin managed to say his prayers.

Love is sleeping in a barn in northern Spain.

30 Tuesday 15 May: Rabanal del Camino to Acebo, 16.5kms

I slept fitfully due to a cold night, not helped by having a cup of tea at nine pm (to warm up) and needing to go to the toilet at around eleven-thirty.

I'm out on the Way around eight, groggy but feeling good after a hot coffee. Despite almost freezing temperature – I can hardly feel my fingers – it has opened up to a glorious, divine day. Not a breath of wind. The wind turbines are silent and I finally manage to catch the sound of the cuckoo on video.

I'm stripping off within half an hour. Just about every ten minutes I need to take a photo, the scenery is so sublime.

The first stop is at about ninety minutes in, at the village of Foncebadón, which feels like it's perched on the side of the hill. A South African couple buys me a fresh OJ. I'm still not sure why I struggle so much to accept gifts like this from people when I have done it myself for others.

As I'm trundling up the hill I imagine the Knights Templar who ensured the safe passage of pilgrims over this mountain back in the twelfth century. The dirt track that I'm following feels like a doorway to the mountains with the trees either side of me.

I figure that Cruz de Ferro is another hour because it's more uphill. But suddenly there it is before me. It hasn't been as steep as I expected or maybe I've been distracted by the scenery. I have a surge of emotion bubble up from my stomach. I can't control it and I don't know where it's come from.

I spot Wanda and Garry up ahead. They're putting things away in their packs and offer to take my photo in front of the cross. I smile my usual smile and remain upbeat but inside I'm in turmoil. Where is this coming from?

I struggle to keep myself together while Garry takes the photo. We chat, then they move on. I look around me and see others hugging and crying. This doesn't help me keep it together, sobs choke in my throat.

Yesterday I planned to do a live video but now I'm much too emotional. I take a photo, and a video but not of myself. I look at the mound of rocks and keepsakes around the base of the cross, which is tall. I think about where to place my stone. I can't bring myself to put it down. I don't think I can. I repeatedly place the stone down only to snatch it up again. It's not in the right spot or I need to think about it more.

I'm crying now and I have no idea why. I don't even know what my thing here is. What am I leaving? Or am I picking up the energy of so many pilgrims who have passed through?

Finally I find a spot to place the stone and take a picture. Tears stream down my face. I lug my pack over to a picnic table and sit there eating a banana and drink copious amounts of water, trying to stem the tears.

I contemplate the large mound of rocks and keepsakes around the base of this cross. Then I watch pilgrims going past. Some stand in contemplation for a long time (some crying and hugging if they're with people), some throw a rock onto the pile and take a selfie, others just march by without a pause. I stay at the picnic table, tears uncontrollable.

Another woman, also emotional, asks if she can sit here. I nod, not trusting my voice. I have my sunglasses on to hide my eyes anyway. We both sit here blowing our noses. She offers me a tissue but I shake my head and hold up my own.

My whole trip has been carried by love, so it's appropriate that I leave my heart stone here, on the Camino. I have carried that from Tralfamadore, across the other side of the world. I guess this means that I'm leaving a piece of my heart on the Camino.

I turn to the lady sitting at the other side of the table and say something about the emotion being a surprise. She starts to cry again. I ask her if she wants a hug and she nods. So here we are, two strangers on the Camino, in a long embrace. Her name is Nicole and she comes from Germany.

So will this mean that I can leave other things, like humiliation, hurt and distrust on this Camino? I'm hoping so. Time to move on. I can only guess that this outpouring of grief is a letting go. And maybe the hesitation about leaving it is the fear of letting go of something that is so much part of my fabric.

Did I mention the glorious day? Here I am in the presence of majesty at 1515 metres. It is divine. Crystal blue sky, no wind. I'm on top of the world with the snow-capped mountains all around me. I now understand the idea of being closer to divinity up here high amongst the trees and sky.

It's still early and I'm light as I leave the mountain and start the slow descent towards my next stop. I pause often to take in my surroundings, taking more photos and video and soaking everything up, listening to cows mooing to each other up and down the hillside.

These rolling hills mentioned in the guidebook are a less rolling than I imagined and there are still many hours of up and down until I come to this cute village called Acebo and the donativo albergue, Apóstol Santiago.

It's around four by the time I get here after some brutal last descents. My poor knees are complaining. Nothing a hot shower and clean clothes won't fix.

This building is pleasant and they are strict about protocols. I feel at home and it reminds me of being back at boarding school.

I find a man in a café that I met yesterday at Rabanal (we sat next to each other for afternoon tea) so I join him and an American woman for a drink. We chat for a while enjoying the afternoon sun. Then I decide to be responsible and go do some washing to make the most of the warm sun.

For dinner it's a shared meal of pasta around the table with about twenty pilgrims. There's lots of joking and laughter and plenty of food and wine, which is all part of the donativo deal. I don't know how much people put in the box but I figure that bed and food is probably worth more than the ten euros that I put in.[85]

To end the spectacular day some of us wander down to the end of the village to where a cross is erected and the sun is sinking behind it. It's been a clear day, which

---

85 Snacks during the day €6.30; albergue (donativo) €10

allows for a spectacular show of colour as the sun sinks slowly to the west.

The only problem with the sunset here is that it's late, around ten, but it's worth the wait despite my tiredness.

What a day.

Love is a hug from a stranger.

31 Wednesday 16 May: Acebo to Columbrianos, 20.4kms

A great sleep, quick breakfast then down the rocky slopes again. Knees have strengthened. It's uneven ground and lots of downwards motion so it's hard work.

I pass Julio and the Dane as I'm trudging through the forest. They walk hand in hand, their packs proudly high on their backs. I sneak a photo of them holding hands.

At around eleven I pass over a medieval bridge into Molinesca and stop at a café for pilgrim cake and café con leche.[86] There's a group of older German women walking together who are boisterous. We chat while waiting for coffee and then I push on.

At around one I approach the city of Ponferrada where I planned to stop but when I finally get here I feel a strong urge not to stay. I approach the old part of the city, up past the impressive Castillo de los Templarios and stop at the Plaza Encina.

---

86 Also called Tarta de Santiago. An almond cake usually decorated with the cross of St James

I'm hot and bothered and my feet are blistering. My pack is heavier than normal. I stop to rest on a park bench and spot the German women from earlier sitting together for lunch.

I can tell that they'd be fine for me to join them but I'm not in the mood for being with people and I don't want to have to try to make conversation.

I'm not even curious enough to linger to look around. I had heard that there's so much to see and it does look beautiful but the bustle is getting to me. I'm feeling lethargic: sore throat, tired. So I rest, have a snack and FaceTime home to catch everyone at open mic night.[87] That's fun but makes me feel homesick.

I haven't talked to anyone about yesterday and I don't know what to do with it. It feels bigger than any conversation that I could have.

So I trudge on. My body is struggling: feet sore, pack heavy, so I stop often. I wonder if I caught this off Wanda a few days ago.

The city pavements go on forever and ever. I opt for the river route out of the city to get away from the traffic and crowds. It's a lovely walk through the Parque de la Concordia and alongside the rio Sil. I sit for a while on another park bench, listening to children

---

87 A monthly night we host at Busybird Publishing

on a playground nearby. My feet are blistering so I take my boots off to inspect them. I'm so low that I start to feel sorry for myself. I can't reconcile how low I feel today after the amazing day I had yesterday.

I stop around three-thirty and sit under a tree to FaceTime Kev before he goes to bed. My eyes are itching and watery.

I finally arrive at the San Blas albergue and am able to stop but it has felt like such a long day. This place is strange but at least I can get a shower and rest.

Julio and his Danish friend are also staying here. They are so cute, sitting next to each other with a glass of red wine, she with lipstick on. They order one meal to share because they can't eat a full pilgrim meal. We chat for a while. I've chatted with them a few times but I don't think they ever remember me.

I have a nap (top bunk), then a pilgrim dinner, then bed. Walk, Eat, Sleep![88]

Love is strong knees.

---

88 Albergue €8; dinner €8.50

32 Thursday 17 May: Columbrianos to Villafranca del Bierzo, 18.8kms

Out of the nine people sleeping in my room last night, EVERYONE snored at some stage. Including myself! I know this because I woke myself with a snort. There is a father and son (Spanish) walking together. The father snores so loudly it's impossible to sleep.

I'm a pure snot-making machine now and it gets hot early. Walking is also on pavements and roads for a big part of the day. I'm happier once we hit the vineyards but it's still up and down hills out in the heat of the sun. I need to stop every half hour.[89]

There's a cute spot under a tree called La Siesta where I buy a wooden cross because I want to support the man who made it.[90] The man at the café won't sell me a banana because they are for the smoothies, so I sit to rest and grumble under my breath. I could sit here for the rest of the day but I push on.

At a tiny village called Valtuille de Arriba, amongst the vineyards, I stop at Cantina Estrella where there's

---

89 I stop for breakfast €3
90 Wooden cross €10

a lovely place to sit under a pergola and listen to music. They only sell drinks, so I have a coke.[91] I badly need food so I nibble on some crackers that I have in my bag.

This place feels totally untouched by time and I listen to other people from the village chatting in Spanish. I'm half dazed from the heat and my cold.

I force myself to continue and walk turtle-slow along farm tracks until finally I arrive at Villa Franca. As I enter the town I pass the Church of Santiago with its entrance facing the Camino. This is the Puerta del Perdon, the place where medieval pilgrims could receive absolution and a compostela if they were unable to continue to Santiago. The town is sometimes called Little Santiago because of this.

I choose to stay at Ave Fenix because it sounds good in the guidebook and my intuition is right.[92] It's one of the oldest albergues on the Camino, owned by the Hato family since the 1930s. The 80-year-old owner is dynamic.

After settling in and having a hot shower I wander down into the town, buy some snacks from the supermarcado. The town is small and bustling. I sit eating a yogurt on a bench and have a conversation with an old Spanish woman, all in Spanish. I have no idea what she says but it's funny.

---

91 €1.50

92 Albergue, includes dinner & breakfast €16; supermarket €5.42

All day, while walking, I had been dreaming of a big bowl of vegetable soup. At dinner, that's what we're served and I have three big bowls of it as well as the rest of the food.

There are about a dozen pilgrims at the table including a family from the US who are homeschooling their kids, William the Texan, and a group of young Spaniards on holiday.

A big storm rolls in and the rain is heavy but I'm safe and sound here in my bottom bunk, cosy and warm.

Love is vegetable soup.

33 Friday 18 May: Villafranca to Herrerías, 20.7kms

I'm always astounded by how different some of the albergues can be in what they offer. This place gives so much value and has heart in it. They grow all their own produce.

Of course the breakfast is a feast: egg on toast, plum jam on toast, and buckets of coffee. I set out around eight, still head clogged but better than yesterday. I'm undecided about which way to go today because there are three options.

One is way too hard for my current health, one is flat but along roads, the other up through the mountains. If my energy levels were better I would have taken the mountains because it sounds beautiful. I opt for the easiest route.[93] I'm still contemplating this as I leave the albergue and pass the impressive Castillo de los Marqueses and down into the town and out the other side.

It's on a paved area a lot but fairly flat, so I make good time. I stop for lunch at Vega: pizza and coffee.[94]

---

93 I deliberate this while drinking fresh orange juice from a wine glass and watching a golden Labrador wait for pats from passing pilgrims €2

94 Lunch €3.20

I had planned to stay in Vega but keep going to the next village, which is at the start of an uphill climb. I'm lucky to get a bed in a place that serves vegetarian food. I'm looking forward to that.

This village is located in a valley and runs along the rio Valcarce. Tomorrow will be a steep climb. Horses are popular here and I overhear people organising horse riding over the ridge. Even during the day a group passed me on horseback trotting through the main street.

I walk around the village but there isn't much to see except the resident cats that come over to rub against my legs. I sit at a bar across the road and order a drink so that I can sit and use their Internet but it isn't worth it. I watch people instead and nod hello to William the Texan as he comes to check in.[95]

Back at the albergue, I find a novel on the shelves that people can take. I haven't read anything for so long that I flick through it greedily. It looks good and is in English. I decide on a siesta in my funny single bed in a corner.

Love is a hearty breakfast.

---

95 Albergue and dinner €16; drink at bar to use Internet €2

34 Saturday 19 May: Herrerías to Fonfria, 20.1kms

The room is full of bunks but luckily I'm in an angled corner in a single bed. I enjoy my cubbyhole at albergue Herreriás and I start a book called *The Muse*.

A heavy shower came down last night as we enjoyed our vegetarian meal with presentation beyond pilgrim standards like platters of slate and earthenware bowls. Beautiful nourishing food.

This is a great place to stay with not too many people although the room too hot for sleeping. I miss my bedroom at home where we sleep with the door open to the backyard.

I knew that today would be a tough climb, and it is. Having a disgusting snotty nose doesn't help but it's a beautiful walk nonetheless. The path winds up through moss-covered tree roots and twisted trees. My energy levels aren't great so I need to stop often.

At O'Cebreiro it's time for breakfast at a bar high up in the mountain. It's bone-chilling cold up here and a heavy mist shrouds the view to the west in the direction

I'm going. The Spaniard at the bar is surly and we're all scared to order breakfast.[96]

The path from here is up and down. I must have legs of steel by now. Despite the low energy, I enjoy this walk through trees and fields and take a selfie at Alto de San Roque where an imposing statue of a medieval pilgrim looks out to the west over the valleys.

I've had enough though by the time I get to Fonfria to Albergue Reboleira, which feels like in the middle of nowhere. This place is huge with three rooms housing sixty-three people each. I don't like the vibe here but I don't have the energy to keep going. There's a youth hostel atmosphere and despite so many people I'm lonely.

There's a good lounge area where I hang out after my shower to write and rest. There's plenty of opportunity to chat to people but I'm not in the mood. I prefer to listen to people's conversations and just observe. At dinnertime we all walk down the hill to another building where we are fed a big feast. There is no way anyone will be hungry after this.[97]

I talk to people on the table around me (William the Texan sits across from me) but my head cold is making it hard to hear and hard to talk, so I leave as early as I

---

96 Breakfast €4. Not everyone in Spain loves pilgrims
97 Albergue €9; dinner €9; Coke €2

can. There are lots of younger people, which is what gave me the youth hostel feel but there are also lots of older people so it's diverse. This is what continually surprises me about the Camino.

Now that I've moved into the land of Galicia, it's as if I've relocated to another country. Gone are the clean villages. They're now carpeted with cow poop and the air is permeated with it (even with a blocked nose). There are chickens, horses, cows, dogs, cats, and old nonnas walking the streets. Tractors are the favoured vehicle.

I take a photo of a shiny blue tractor that is parked in a glass house that looks like it should store plants but there's this tractor gleaming in the sunshine like a trophy.

Love is a good book.

35 Sunday 20 May: Fonfria to Samos, 19.3kms

This cold has taken hold of me now but I opt for the scenic route, despite it being six-point-five kilometres longer.[98] It's worth it to walk along rio Oribio, through the old forest. It's hard going because I'm low on energy. It must be every twenty or thirty minutes that I need to stop but it's lovely and quiet. I hardly see anyone and when I do I feel like they are on my path. Time stands still in the old forest. I pass old derelict buildings and graveyards, and pathways lined with dry-stone walls.

I approach Samos from above and admire the monastery nestled amongst the trees below. When I finally arrive in the gorgeous hamlet it's to be confronted by the monastery in the middle of the town. There are beautiful ornate shells all over the town – made from wrought iron – like shell-shaped garbage bins, as well as decorative shells on the rails of the bridge.

It's picturesque and despite the size of the monastery it has a nestled feel about it that makes me

---

98 Breakfast is at a bar a few kilometres along the Way €4

think that it has been here a long time. There are ducks on the river that runs down one side of it and a bridge crossing over. It's straight out of a fairy tale.

The first thing I need is food; it's already long after lunchtime and I'm depleted. While I wait for it, I call Kev. Then I eat my tortilla, which restores me quickly, while looking out over the monastery.

I shuffle over to the Monasterio de Samos and check in. I don't know too much about the history of it except that it's one of the oldest monasteries in Europe, founded in the Benedictine faith in the sixth century.

It's one big, cold room that sleeps seventy pilgrims. I wonder if it's a mistake to stay here but I need sleep. I'm also given a top bunk with no ladder or rails, so I'm worried about falling out or needing to go to the toilet in the night. On the upside, it's a donativo and I don't have energy to find something else.

Once I shower and sort out my bed, there isn't much to do in the room. I can't sit on my bed and there's no lounge area. I wander around Samos. It is so pretty and the monastery is imposing at all angles. Behind it at the end of the town is a small chapel, Capilla Ciprés S. Salvador IXth. It's literally a chapel with a cypress tree growing next to it. Legend says that if you touch the cypress tree, you will remain blister free. I never need an excuse to hug a tree.

Since I had a late lunch and I'm not hungry, I opt for just a hot black tea across the road late in the day. It's still daylight so it's not actually that late. I find some throat lozenges but no luck with headache tablets because it's Sunday and the only place open is a tiny general store.

I go to bed fully clothed, in my sleeping bag with the heavy horse blanket they provide. William the Texan has the bunk underneath me. He's exactly as you would expect a Texan to be: tall, lanky, with a long face and long drawling accent. He's about sixty-five and polite.

I try not to move too much because this old bunk squeaks and groans every time I do. It's barely dark but plenty of people are ready for bed and thankfully the lights are out by ten.

The room fills with snores almost immediately. I prepare for a long night as I shuffle as close to the wall as I can so that I don't fall off the bunk onto the floor about a metre-and-a-half down.

I'm so tired that I fall asleep quickly, snug in my cocoon.[99]

Love is a good sleep.

---

99 Monastery bed (donativo) €5; lunch, drinks, lozenges €8.90

36 Monday 21 May: Samos to Sarria, 14.8kms

I sleep long and deep, hardly moving all night and only waking because there is rustling and movement in the dark around me. William whacks his head on the metal railing of the bunk as he bends to pack his sleeping bag. He swears under his breath: *God darn it!*

Despite the great sleep I'm still sluggish. My chest is tight and my head clogged. I plan a short day because Sarria is close.

It's a beautiful walk out of Samos despite my lethargy. The Way starts on the main road but soon crosses over and disappears into woodlands. The old forest is straight out of Brothers Grimm, stepping over twisted roots covered in green moss and a heavy canopy of branches overhead. It's dark and mysterious and I half expect some mythical creature to appear before me.

At my first rest stop I sit on the step of a tiny wayside chapel in Gorolfe. There's no one around and I hear scurrying nearby. I figure it must be a fox or something but then I spot two creatures running together playfully. They are small and kitten-like with a white stripe down the middle. My first thought is that they are skunks but I don't think they're native to Spain, so I make a note to find out what they are.[100] I reach for my camera but they scurry under cover before I can capture them. I sit still for a long time in the hope that they return but all I hear is the whispering wind in the nearby forest.

There's a tunnel that comes out at the village of Hospital and the path rejoins the main Camino. There are lots of pilgrims again. I stop here for a snack and toilet stop, happy that I'd taken the detour.[101]

I arrive in Sarria around lunchtime and find a great albergue called Casa Peltre. I know that resting for half a day will help me. There aren't many people here yet so I enjoy the peace, have a long hot shower in a private bathroom, wash some clothes and go in search of food.

I eat a big vegetable paella, just ordering it before they close the kitchen for siesta. Then I find a supermarket and some headache tablets, honey, and a lemon. I bump into an Argentinian guy with his mum. I've seen them at lots of places now. They're walking a similar pace to me but I don't talk to them much and just say hi.

---

100 I asked Spanish people about these creatures but had trouble explaining myself. I'm guessing they were weasels.
101 Toilet stop, breakfast €4

The American in the bunk next to me is walking on his own because his wife told him he had to. I giggle to myself about this because I know why she wants him to and he is perturbed by it even though he's close to the end. They're meeting in Santiago in a few days. I wonder if he's learned the things that his wife hopes he will?

It feels rude but I'm close to finishing my book so I sit to read it in the communal lounge. It's hard to stay quiet because an English couple, Hugh and Mary, sit nearby and ask me lots of questions. I learn that they're brother and sister. I find them overly friendly and I raise my guard straight away. There's that distrust lurking deep inside me. We chat for a while and then I get to finish my book.[102]

Love is walking through a forest.

---

102 Albergue €10; washing €3; late lunch €13.50; supermarket €6; tea €1.30

37 Tuesday 22 May: Sarria to Portomarin, 22.7kms

I wake up and my cold isn't as debilitating. Maybe the lemon and honey drink helped. My chest isn't as inflamed. I'm now almost to the last one hundred-kilometre mark, which is surreal.

Sarria is the last starting point for pilgrims who want to get a compostela in Santiago. You must complete one hundred kilometres to obtain one. We also need to get two stamps in our pilgrim passport each day instead of one.

After a quick breakfast in a bar, I pass the ruins of the Sarria castle Fortaleza de Sarria. I can't help take a photo of an old door that looks childlike in design. It's at the church of St. Saviour and the door has a primitive Romanesque tympanum above it and is a rich red.

The city has so much to look at that I wish I could stay longer but I'm getting so close to the end. It's feeling touristy now and I have to fight the crowds on the Way, past the stone crucerio with the view over the city. It's hard to get a good view because everyone is taking selfies with the monument. Finally there's the cemetery and Capela de San Lazaro across the road to rio Celeiro and over the medieval Ponte Áspera (rough bridge). It's hard to get good photos of the bridge because of the hordes of people.

The path out of Sarria is steep and misty and my energy levels are still low, so it's hard going but good. It's hard not to be critical about these groups of people with their brand new walking shoes and daypacks, stepping off big buses on tour. I'm sure many of them pre-booked their accommodation too.[103]

You can see the difference in the faces of these pilgrims compared to the more seasoned ones. The newbies are all excited and energetic and taking selfies and group photos in front of every monument they come across. It's hard not to let it press against the peaceful bubble that has formed around me over the last month or so.

The walk is picturesque. Heavy mist hangs low until around eleven-thirty and then it clears to a bright blue and warm day. Just about every café is bustling with people and it's like a day at Disneyland. In a way it's probably good to start easing out of the state I'm in so that I can integrate back into a normal life.[104]

---

103 Breakfast is at a bar on the Way €3.80 (toilet stop)
104 Lunch is at another bar €6.50 (also toilet stop)

I arrive at Albergue de Portomarin in Portomarin around four, so it's a long day but I'm happy with the progress after feeling so crappy for days. The cold has definitely broken. This albergue is large and modern with a big kitchen but strangely enough there's nothing in the kitchen to cook or eat with, which makes me think they want you to go eat at one of the restaurants.

I have a big bowl of carbonara and a tinto de verano for dinner.[105]

Now I'm waiting for a reasonable time to go to bed. The Argentian and his mother are here as well as other people who are familiar but I haven't spoken to them. Mostly it's a nod hello as we pass each other.

I'm not sure how many bunks are in my room but they are squeezed in tight and you are up against another bunk so too bad if you don't want to be close to a stranger.

Love is practising patience.

---

105 Albergue €6; dinner with wine €12; snack €1; tinto de verano is red wine mixed with lemonade and means 'red wine of summer'

38 Wednesday 23 May: Portomarin to Palas de Rei, 24.6kms

The albergue was hot and full of snorers and people who started shuffling bags at five-thirty this morning!

Since I'm awake and the light gets turned on around six, I may as well get up. I'm out the door by six-forty five. Out into the dark fog, which doesn't lift until about eleven.

The Camino is so busy now that the joy of it is gone and my pack is heavy. I guess it's a way of re-integrating back into some kind of normal existence. I try to talk myself into being back in civilisation or real life and that what's happening now will help me but the chattering of people around me is extremely annoying. Even in the fog I can't see more than a few metres ahead but I can hear people talking all around me – it's dreamlike.[106]

There's plenty of uphill slog but there's so much to see and it's picturesque, with plenty of places to stop for food. I'm guessing that because we're into the last dash to Santiago that the Camino is catering for all the extra pilgrims.

---

106 Cooked breakfast €6.50; drinks & supermarket €7; albergue €10

I stop at Gonzar for breakfast and get talking to three German women who're walking together. They're fascinated by the fact that I'm on my own. They ask me copious questions while chain-smoking and drinking lots of coffee.

I planned to stay in an albergue in Portos, called A Paso de Formiga (Ants' Nest) but it's full. I should've guessed this since there are so many people about and many of them are pre-booking. As well as that this place has only eight beds.

I'm very disappointed so I sit on a stone wall to rest a while and pout. I sip from my water bottle and eat a banana.

It's another hour of walking to Palas de Rei. I'm over it by the time I arrive – especially my aching feet. But the San Marcos Albergue is fabulous and there are only seven people in the room. So once I'm showered and have washed some socks I'm good again. I sit outside at a table in the sun and write and nibble on snacks.

The kitchen is well-equipped so I search out a store to buy ingredients for pasta because I'd rather spend the money in Santiago when I see Marg on Sunday night. I can't believe that I'm only seventy kilometres from the end.

Love is clean socks.

39 Thursday 24 May: Palas de Rei to Boente, 21kms

I'm slow to start. Breakfast is good here so I eat as much as I can so early in the morning.[107] I think the impending end is making me reluctant to move forward because, while I'm ready to go home, I'm also lamenting the end of this amazing journey.

There are fewer people today and it's a pleasant start through tree-lined roads. No fog means it's warm early and I'm sweaty by ten. Then swarms of people appear. Bus loads in fact. That bursts my bubble but then I stop for lunch at about midday at a restaurant with lots of outdoor tables (I recognise many faces as I walk in).

I see Mary and Hugh who were at the Sarria albergue and they decide to have lunch with me. I think that they're fascinated by Australia. I have to admit that I'm wary of them because they are so familiar and friendly. My first response to this is that they are after something, like maybe an invitation to Australia? I'm not sure and I feel guilty having these thoughts.

I have a spectacular salad with goat cheese. It's

---

107 Breakfast €4

expensive but it sounds so tasty that I can't resist. As I talk with Hugh and Mary I decide that they are lovely people and it's civilised sitting here learning about each other over food. The Camino does this.

As we leave, Hugh sneaks off and pays the bill and won't let me pay. I'm embarrassed, especially after the suspicious thoughts that I had earlier. I'm humbled. We hug and go our separate ways.

About thirty minutes later, after walking along eucalyptus-lined pathways, I come to the crossing of rio Lazaro. It could easily be the Wadbilliga River in New South Wales.[108] My heart flutters. The same crystal clear water and smooth pebbled stones at the bottom. The same river where my heart shaped stone came from.

Mary and Hugh are there with their shoes off and feet in the water. Other pilgrims are doing the same. Of course I have to do it after twenty seconds of hesitation; it's getting late in the day. The water is clear and deadly cold. So good. I stay here long after Mary and Hugh have moved on.

After drying my feet and putting my trusty boots back on, my feet are invigorated and I waft along the pathway with the scent of eucalyptus, the deep-throated frogs and the twitter of birds all around me.

---

108 A river from my childhood home

I arrive at Boente just after three and check into Albergue Boente, which is literally on the Way, and settle in for the night. This place is good, with rooms above the bar. I chat with people and am sleeping near the same three German women who are travelling together. They ask me more questions about walking alone. Am I lonely? Do I feel safe? They tell me I've inspired them but I don't see what I've done as unique. I've seen plenty of women and men of all ages do exactly the same on the Camino.[109]

Apparently a storm is brewing.

Only fifty clicks to go.

Love is a crystal clear river.

---

109 Albergue €10; dinner €10; coffee €1.30

40 Friday 25 May: Boente to Pedrouzo, 29kms

It rained heavily last night so this morning is damp and fresh, bringing out the scent of eucalyptus all around me. It brings up nostalgia for me.

I'm not sure where all the crowds have gone but I find myself alone many times throughout the day. The walking conditions are perfect all day, if a bit steamy at times.[110]

I plan to stay at Salceda and arrive around two but it feels too early to stop; I'm feeling strong and love walking in this weather. I keep going.

The next place I think about stopping at is Santa Irene but it's on a very busy road, so I don't fancy it. I keep walking.

I arrive at Pedrouzo around four, still feeling good but the day is crowding in and a light drizzle is constant and cold. I check in to Albergue Edeira, which is cosy and big with good amenities and fabulous hot showers.

---

110 Breakfast €2.50 (with toilet stop). I'm joined by the German trio who smoke like chimneys

For dinner I walk into town and have a vegetarian meal that is pricey but hearty and the atmosphere is trendy.[111]

And now I only have twenty kilometres to go! Santiago is tomorrow. Is it true? Just like a good book, I've moved forward, wanting to get to the end but now that it's nearing, I am lamenting it.

Love is the scent of eucalyptus.

---

111 Albergue €10; snacks & drinks €6.50; dinner €15

41 Saturday 26 May: Pedrouzo to Santiago, 20.1kms

It rained again during the night but has eased by the time I leave at seven. I lose about twenty minutes going to the other end of the town before realising that the albergue is close to the Way. It doesn't matter. This is the final day of walking, so naturally I'm in a fantastic mood. Nothing much can bring me down today.[112]

The rain has made the eucalyptus ever present again and the first couple of hours are lovely and quiet, walking through eucalyptus forest with the scent permeating the air.

It's a decent hike up to the top of Monte de Gonzo and there are other pilgrims about but not the crowds of the last few days. I don't know where they've gone. It's cold and dreary today. A light drizzle makes me keep moving to keep warm.

Finally there it is: Santiago.

I stop to take a selfie at the sign that says 'Santiago'.

---

112 Breakfast at a diner-like restaurant €4.80 (it's getting more expensive as I approach Santiago)

There's a festive feeling rising around other pilgrims as we close in on the centre of the city.

For some reason I need to delay arriving at the Cathedral. I stop at a bar for lunch.[113]

From the bar I watch pilgrims walking, most with their packs but one young woman has a cart hooked up to her waist like my Argentian friends. I wonder what they're all thinking and feeling. I'm not sure what I'm thinking or feeling myself.

And, suddenly, I'm in the square in front of the Cathedral. Am I here? At first I'm not sure if this is it but I spot some familiar people and offer to take their photo, then they take mine.

I'm out of kilter, not knowing what I should be thinking or doing.

I'm here!

I sit on a stone bench to one side and watch people walking into the square. Elation, laughter, group hugs. It feels lonely not to share this with someone. I call Kev and burst into tears when I start talking to him.

I'm here!

And then what do you do when you've walked over eight hundred kilometres over six weeks? It's hard to know. The first thing I need to do is find a bed before too many people arrive.

---

113 Coffee & cake €5 (with toilet stop)

The first albergue I try is *completo*, then the second, Roots and Boots, the girl isn't sure. I pray under my breath that there is a bed and yes! 'Cris had booked but is no longer coming'. So I'm now in a groovy albergue on the bottom bunk with spacious bathrooms and a short walk to the city centre. The Camino has provided.

I enjoy a lovely, long hot shower, wash my hair and leave some clothes with the front desk to be washed. It's still early so I decide that I may as well go and line up for my credential.

I have time to wait, after all!

The wait is long and my feet and calves ache over that hour-and-a-half. It's as if I need the forward motion for my feet to not ache.

So now I have my credential and the walk is done. It's too early to articulate how I feel or anything about it.[114] They say that when you walk the Camino, getting to the end is just the beginning.

Then a friend, Tess from Melbourne, messages me and I join her and her group for dinner at a Tapas bar. I have a gorgeous meal of salmon and grilled vegetables. They are all staying at the place that I will be checking into tomorrow. It's interesting to hear their Camino story because they had a two-week walk on the Portuguese route not carrying packs and having

---

114 Credential with tube €5

all accommodation sorted for them. Tess did have back surgery last year and is close to seventy, so fair enough. I'm excited that I've been able to catch them on their last night in Spain.

Love is arriving.

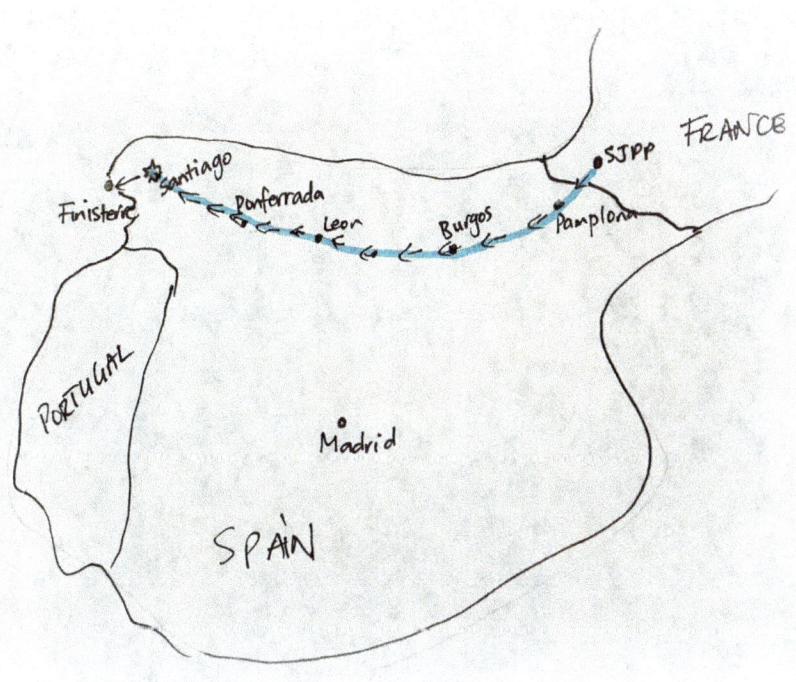

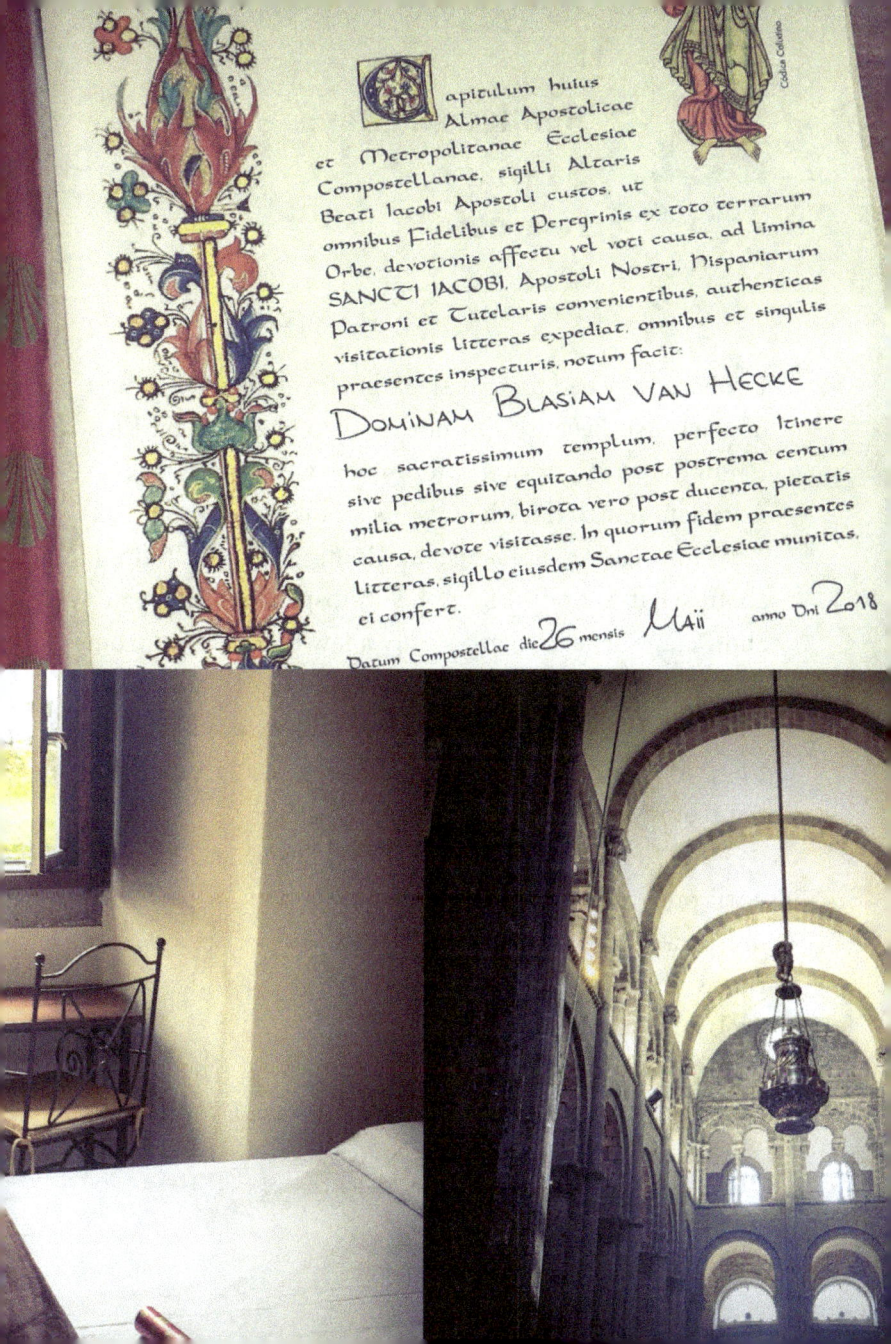

42 Sunday 27 May: Santiago, rest day

I'm here ... I had a good sleep in the albergue but was up early-ish because I'm not used to sleeping in. Plus I now have my period after seven weeks.[115] I was so fortunate not to have had it this whole time.

While eating breakfast at Roots & Boots, I think about what to do.[116] I love the atmosphere in this place and I can't believe that it's only a few blocks away from the centre of the old part of Santiago. I also can't believe that I'm here and that I just finished walking all this way by myself. I'm now only days away from flying out from Madrid.

I can't check into San Marino Pinaro (San Martiño) until one but I'm guessing that they will let me leave my pack there until later. I check out of Roots and Boots at nine and head over to see if I can leave my pack and, yes, I can.

So, now free of the burden of my bag, I head back to the pilgrim information centre for a map. I walk past

---

115 I'm coming into menopause and cycles are non-existent
116 Breakfast €4

the line of pilgrims lining up for their credential and who should I meet but Mary and Hugh from Ireland. They're near the start of the queue, so I suggest we have coffee. I take photos of them both with their pilgrim certificates.

We only have a short amount of time, so we have a quick coffee in the main street, then we walk to the Cathedral for the pilgrim midday mass.

The cathedral is packed, so we don't get a seat but that's okay. I lose Mary and Hugh almost straight away amongst the crowd so I opt for a spot next to a column so that I can lean against it. I'm guessing there're about a thousand people here. The mass goes for an hour and my legs ache; I'm even feeling woozy. I don't think my body likes being still.

They don't swing the incense burner until the end and it's swinging the opposite way to where I'm standing. I'm not engaging in the ceremony. Most of the mass is in Spanish, so it's lost on me and I guess I'm just tired and need to rest. It has been a big adventure.

After the mass I check into San Martiño, which is an old monastery. The rooms are nuns' cells. The luxury of sleeping between white sheets will be special tonight and I have my own toilet and shower. I can't wait. It's five star compared to what I've been staying in.

My friend Margaret Caffyn from Australia arrives today and is only a few rooms down the hall. It will be great seeing another familiar face and especially good to hang out with someone who knows this city well.

When she arrives we go walking and she shows me some of her favourite places – the cafes where the locals go – and we sit out in a courtyard and catch up over coffee. After a while, her Spanish taxi-driver friend, Gonzo, turns up. We talk a while, then I'm in need of a nap. I'm drained now and looking forward to having some time out. It's still early in the day. My period is also heavy, so I need some more tampons.

Turns out that tampons are hard to find on a Sunday afternoon in Spain. The supermarket is closed when I go back and I was only there this morning. I finally find some with the awful applicators in a convenience store and they are twice the price that they should be.

Around seven, after a nap, I message Marg to see what we are doing for dinner. I don't hear from her for an hour and by then I'm starving. I'm still not used to Spanish meal-times, even after six weeks, and I have been up since around seven.

She eventually turns up at eight-thirty and we trundle off to have Italian. At the front of the restaurant is Julio and the Dane looking gorgeous and well after their Camino. I quietly pledge to be like them in my 70s.

The food is hearty and sustains me. It's so great to catch up with Marg and to hear about her latest Camino. I've lost count of how many different ones she's done now. She's leaving early in the morning to fly to Madrid, then France to catch up with someone else and do some more walking, I think.[117]

Love is a shared meal with a friend.

---

[117] Tampons €5; dinner with wine €20; coffee €2

43 Monday 28 May: Santiago to Finisterre, 30kms

I had the chance to sleep in but can't thanks to fat pillows and a heavy period. Blahhh!

At least I have the privacy of my own room and can check out at twelve. I get up, shower, then head off to breakfast downstairs. Afterwards I search for real tampons at the supermarket, which I do find.

Now I have to decide my next moves. I consider staying in Santiago. I ask if my room is free for tonight but the whole place is fully booked. That's probably just as well because it doesn't fit my budget even though it isn't terribly expensive. I don't think that I've been so indecisive the whole time I've been on this trip. I'm unmoored.

Originally, I was going to walk from Santiago down to Finisterre but I don't have the energy for it now. I'm wasting time trying to decide what to do. I wander aimlessly around Santiago. It's a beautiful bustling city.

I go to the post office to retrieve the package that I sent from Torres del Rio on day eight, so many weeks ago. I'm surprised that it's actually there and they haven't given up on me picking it up.

Finally I decide that I'll go to Cee by bus. Mike from England had suggested this was a good idea because there isn't much between here and Cee. This feels like a plan. I book two nights in a pension in Finisterre and decide I'll wing it for tonight once I get to Cee.

I check out of San Martiño and start heading towards the bus station.[118] I'm not sure when it goes to Cee so I drop by the pilgrim house on my way. Lucky I do because the bus is in the opposite direction to where I was heading. They also hint that there isn't much to see in Cee.

So I bolt to the bus station, fully loaded with a pack and make the bus with five minutes to spare. I ride a moving vehicle for the first time in six weeks, headed for Finisterre.[119]

I arrive at Finisterre around three but my accommodation is booked for tomorrow, so I need to find something for just tonight. I find a great albergue with full kitchen and only one person in my room. So, in view of the kitchen, I head straight out to the supermarcado and stock up on salad, fruit, pasta and have a big cook up.

---

118 Room & breakfast €82

119 Bus from Santiago to Finisterre takes 90 mins €10

Finisterre is a gorgeous seaside village and I'm so glad that I'm staying here for a few days. The other woman in my room, Val from the US, told me about a boat trip to see the sunset so I decide to take it.

The sunset cruise is lovely and romantic.[120] I wish that Kev were with me. There's a German man onboard who asks me out to dinner. I'm thankful that I have already eaten and it's already after ten thanks to the late sunset here. It's eleven by the time I snuggle into my sleeping bag with a contented sigh.[121]

Love is a Spanish sunset.

---

120 I buy the ticket in the afternoon €15, includes wine & nibbles
121 Albergue €10; supermarket €25; vending machine €1

44 Tuesday 29 May: Finisterre, contemplation

After breakfast I check out the town and decide what to do for the day. I'm strangely lost without the rhythm of the Camino. I ask to leave my pack at the albergue and walk down to the water. The water looks inviting but I'm sure it's cold. There are lots of people collecting shells and enjoying looking around a clothes market on the marina.

As I'm walking along the marina, looking at boats and people, I spot someone who looks familiar in the distance. Edda!

We both started in SJPP on the same day and saw each other from time to time along the way. But I haven't seen her for a while. I was hoping to see her before I left Spain but had decided that I wouldn't now that I'd left Santiago.

So we have coffee, then go to Praia do mar de Fora once I've checked into my pension (my own room plus bathroom!).[122]

We spend a couple of hours on that pristine beach (to the west of Finisterre), laughing about how we

---

[122] Pension Cabo €56 for two nights (highly recommended)

survived the Camino. We talk about the things that we learned about ourselves and what our life might be like when we return home. Only one or two people come and go while we're there looking out to the west as we have done for the past six weeks.

The end of the Earth.

When we get back to town we go for food at a German restaurant and have beer and schnitzel.[123] So good. By now it's about four, so we hug goodbye (until tomorrow) and I go to my room where I have the longest, hottest shower – bliss!

My own room.

I quickly spread out all my stuff. There are actually two single beds in the room so I can make myself at home and watch people go by in the street below as the sea waves at me from down the hill.

I had planned to walk to the lighthouse tomorrow but it's still sunny and I don't want to risk that tomorrow might not be as nice so I walk up to the end of the world. It's about seven-thirty by the time I get up there after a forty-five minute walk.

I take lots of photos and videos. It takes three attempts at asking different people to take a picture of me at the zero counter. Each one of them is at a weird angle but at least I have a picture – proof that I was there.

---

123 Dinner with beer €14

I had planned to burn my plane ticket in the fire pit but once I get there I see others having solemn ceremonies and I feel like I've done all the purging that I need to do. None of my trauma is anything like losing a child or spouse, as many of them seem to be. In fact, any of my suffering is mild in the scheme of things.

The problem with waiting for the sun to set is that it's a long wait. I sit for about ninety minutes, sitting on the rocks, facing west, gazing at an endless sea. Birds glide around in circles above me and I watch a couple having a picnic nearby. It looks a like a romantic time, and I imagine that there's a proposal happening. It's hard to not feel romantic in this setting.

I imagine days gone by when the Druids made their rituals here as the sun sank into the sea. How many other religions have made their own rituals in this place? It's impossible to not feel inspired by the energy and spirit of the surroundings.

I walk back down into Finisterre in the dark, the lights coming on in buildings and churches making interesting architecture. I fall asleep in my own room, tired and happy.

Love is schnitzel and beer.

45 Wednesday 30 May: Finisterre, rest day

The end of the world.

This is the place that the body of Saint James was meant to come so many years ago but marauders set upon the apostles and they had to leave his body in the place that is now Santiago. It does feel like the end of the world here, this sleepy fishing village.

I enjoy a long sleep in, waking around nine, and mooch around my room until about midday. I'm so lazy! I decide that I should enjoy my last day in this sweet village so I head out to Praia de San Roque, the long beach that I can see from town that faces east. I walk along the beach barefooted. The water is chilly and clear. I collect some shells to take home. They're the same as any shells I would find in Australia but these ones are from the end of the world. As I'm shuffling along the sand, there's Edda again. We plan coffee in the afternoon.

On my way back to my room I stop by a shop that sells bags and homewares (like a two-dollar shop) to grab a cheap backpack. As I'm coming out I bump into the Italians. We laugh and catch up and take a photo of the three of us. I tell them to visit me if they ever come to Australia.

I call home, write in my journal, eat a sandwich, then meet Edda for coffee and cheesecake. We joke again about how we survived the Camino, how we've suffered, then we laugh as if it's the funniest thing we've ever said. We talk about our lives back home. Edda's English is good but she isn't confident about it. We take photos together and wish each other a good life. I promise her that I will send her a copy of this book when it's done.

As I head back to my room I see the three German women at a café smoking and drinking coffee. They're waiting for their bus back to Santiago. One of them tells me I've inspired her to walk the whole Camino on her own. I wish her luck.

Despite a chilly overcast start for the day it has turned into patchy sun but mild. I'm starting to be sad about having to leave. It's been restful here but I'm also looking forward to going home. I have one last goodbye at the westerly beach on my own before coming back to my room to get ready for an early bus.[124]

Love is sand between your toes.

---
124 Trinkets €20; coffee & cake €10; coffee €1.40

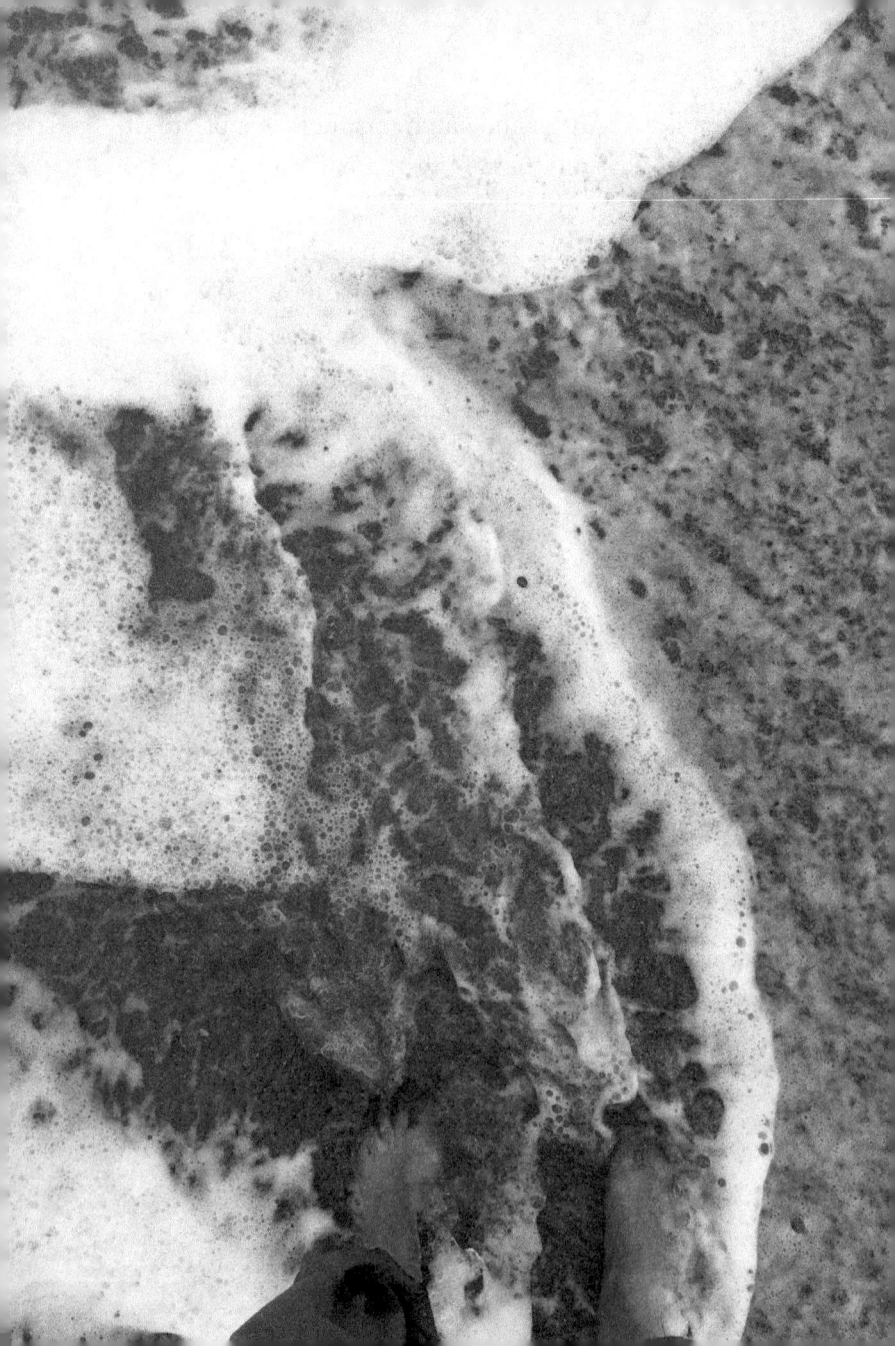

46 Thursday 31 May: Finesterre to Santiago, (bus)

I get the early bus right outside the place where I've been staying and the trip goes quickly talking to an American man the whole way.[125] It's only about an hour anyway, much quicker than coming down for some reason. I remember that I was going to walk this part and it would take me three or four days.

I check into Roots and Boots so I can leave my bag, then spend the day taking photos and playing tourist. Eating breakfast, buying gifts for people back home.[126]

I love Santiago. It's a city full of history and interesting architecture and the people are friendly.

At four I head over to Pilgrim House for the pilgrim debrief. This debrief is much more intense than I had anticipated and even though there is just the group leader and two other pilgrims, there's a lot to talk about and we are all in tears by the end of it – not sad tears but emotion for all this big experience that we've gone through. It's hard to articulate any of it.

---

125 Bus €10

126 Albergue €16; breakfast €5; earrings €20; museum €1.20; poster & bracelet €8; leather bag €25; drinks €2; dinner €25; t-shirt & scarf €38

Everyone warns us about 'getting back to reality'. It's hard to know what they mean by this but I park that for future reference. Do I have a plan? No. I wouldn't know how to make one. But one thing I've learned on this trip is to trust the universe. As I leave Pilgrim House, I bump into the Italians again! They are so lovely. We laugh and hug again.

I go back to the Italian restaurant that I went to on Saturday night with Maggie and enjoy a glass of rioja red wine. So easy to drink.

I finally find the pilgrim museum, which is interesting and half price for pilgrims. I'm now back at the albergue and will have to plan my escape from the top bunk at four tomorrow morning without waking anyone.

Love is getting ready for home.

47 Friday 1 June: Santiago to Madrid, 602kms

There's a light drizzle as I slip out of Roots and Boots at four. It's still dark. The cobblestones are slick with rain and the city lights reflect in small puddles. It's cold but it doesn't take me long to warm up. I'm at the train station in about twenty minutes.

There are groups of revelers still up from the night before and I'm self-conscious with my big pack and hiking clothes. I'm happy to make it to the train. I'm in second class this time, a cheaper ticket, but I can't see any difference in the quality of the carriage. The train is full, and fast. This is one of those fast trains and it's about five hours to Madrid.[127] I doze on and off, watching Spanish shows and people around me.

At the Madrid central train station I stop to eat before tackling the streets to look for my pension. I'm starving and tired.

I head back to Gran Via where I stayed when I was in Madrid at the beginning. I find Pension Berti Madrid, which is just across the road from the underground train station, and McDonalds.

---

127 Second class ticket €33.80

My room has no windows.[128] It's nothing like the images online and I'm disappointed. When I close the door it's pitch black and there's no air. It's claustrophobic. At least I have a sink but the bathrooms are shared and you can hear everything that's happening in the building.

I know this place is cheap but I stayed in better places along the Camino that cost almost nothing. I wonder how I'm going to stand this place for two nights.

The shower is at least cleansing – I'm not fussed about sharing – it cools me down as well. Then I head out to look at the shops and play tourist. I have only one full day left in Spain and I'm feeling a mix of excitement at going home but sadness that my trip is ending.

I'm not enamoured by Madrid but it could be that the big city is too intense for me right now and that I have been looking at old buildings for the last six weeks. It's hot and busy and makes me anxious.

I look for gifts for people back home but most of it is junk so I don't buy much – just tokens of Spain that will be meaningless to anyone back home.

I'm in need of a massage but all I can find is an Asian place like we have back home. I opt for a foot massage but the woman isn't good and I regret getting

---

128 Booked on booking.com, €60 for two nights, not recommended

it. They talk amongst themselves in a language I don't understand and all I can think of is the *Seinfeld* episode where Elaine gets a manicure and the women talk about her without her knowing.

In my last day, I wonder what I can do that is quintessential to Spain. I don't have the energy to go on a tour or visit galleries so I decide on a Flamenco show. Thanks to Google, it's easy enough to find something close and I book it for tomorrow night.

I search out a place to eat paella across at Gran Via. The waiter doesn't like giving me a table for one but he does. It's out on the street, which I like because it's warm and I can watch people walking by. It's bustling and with people from all over the world.[129]

> *Love is wet cobblestones in a*
> *medieval city before dawn.*

---

129 Massage €10; Flamenco show €28; dinner €20 with wine

48 Saturday 2 June: Madrid, last day

I sleep in as much as I can after the big day yesterday. As I'm heading back out to Gran Via for breakfast, I bump into my Argentinian friends. I love this couple. They hardly speak any English but they are so with it in terms of communicating. We take a photo of the three of us and say a final goodbye.

I have a big cooked breakfast in the restaurant underneath Praktik Metropol (I wish I had stayed there again) and contemplate my day. I'm flying home tomorrow!

How will I fill the day? I window shop for a while but all the shops are the usual ones just like we have back home. I've never been a shopper. I call home to chat to Kev, who's hanging out to have me home. He'll pick me up from the airport.

Since I'm going to a Flamenco show tonight, I figure that I should have red-painted nails so I use the trusty Google to find a nail salon. I find one but they don't speak English. We agree on what I want using hand gestures but I've never seen someone so bored with their job or so disinterested in giving a service. The girl is on her mobile phone a lot of the time while doing my nails.

Around lunchtime I'm starving so I find a Japanese place. It's a set menu and such a change from the food that I've been eating.

The show is a seven-thirty session and includes a glass of wine. I dress as well as I can given what clothes I have: silk skirt with hiking sandals is a strange combination but I do have my scarf, which makes me feel the part.

The show is fantastic and energetic. I'm sorry that it only goes for about an hour. It's just as I expected, men and women on stage in colourful costumes and fast-paced guitars and stomping feet.[130]

I go back to my room and repack my bag for the last time. I'm worried about not waking up in the morning and I can't tell the time of day or night in my room. It's oppressive and I know I won't really sleep anyway. I try to doze as much as possible.

> *Love is the opportunity to see Flamenco performers in Madrid.*

---

130 Red nails €18; lunch €10

CARDAM

49 Sunday 3 June: Madrid to Melbourne, endless hours

As I step out into the street from my hotel I get a rush of fresh air. It's just getting light and the streets are bustling with people. Surely people don't get up this early on a Sunday? Then I realise that they haven't gone home yet as I step over rubbish and around two men locked in a deep kiss.

I was expecting quiet streets but feel more relaxed with all this activity around me. I had considered taking a taxi but I've studied the train route and am confident that I'll get to the airport with the three hours required before departure. The station is just around the corner and only a few stops to the central station and then out to the airport.

I'm right about the train but the size of the airport astounds me. It takes almost as long to find the right terminal, then walk a long way to get to the right check-in counter. I'm tired by the time I check in and happy to offload my pack, which must now weigh about ten kilos.

Now I just wait for my flight and the many hours in the air before I get back to my beloveds. I check in with Kev for the last time before my flight.

Love is being loved and missed.

50 Monday 4 June: In the air

The Spanish people are so friendly. The contrast is obvious when I get off at Abu Dhabi for my connecting flight to Melbourne. The people at this airport are rude and unfriendly so it isn't so pleasant to have to wait a few hours between flights.

But what an adventure I've had. And I got exactly what I came for even though I didn't know what that was till a few days ago.

I'm like Dorothy. I always knew what I know but I had to re-find it. It's time to tap my heels together (hiking boots). There's no place like home, there's no place like home ...

The flight home from Europe is almost as epic as walking across Spain! Not exactly, but an hour delay makes it feel excruciatingly long.

I'm looking forward to sleeping in my own bed tonight after being in about forty-six different beds!

There's a quote I have on my fridge at home by Nelson Mandela: *It always seems impossible until it's done.* I've proven that to myself in so many ways. It's amazing where you can go simply by putting one foot in front of the other.

I'm also fully aware of the many blessings that I have and the love that has carried me across Spain for the last fifty days. It would not have been possible without that support.

Love is being home where my heart is.

Postscript

In the days, weeks, months after my return from Spain, many people asked me what I had learned from the trip. The question was always too big to answer and it took a long time to process. I felt full to bursting with newfound knowledge about myself, life, other people. It felt too much to harness into sentences so I stayed mute. I felt changed but it was hard to assimilate back into a 'normal' life afterwards.

I'm hopeful that this account of my walk answers the question of how it changed me. The truth is, it did not actually change me. It was a rediscovery of all the things that I had forgotten about myself and that I am everything I need. I am good enough.

Most of all, it reminded me that the answer to everything is: LOVE. Relearn to love yourself and the rest will follow. Trust that the universe will provide anything else that you need – a good pair of boots is helpful.

I recommend anyone of any age to walk the Camino, but beware, it gets under your skin. Buen Camino!

Camino List

For anyone planning to walk the Camino, the less you carry the better. This is an opportunity to learn how little you need. It is suggested that 10 per cent of your body weight is ideal. My pack was not the ideal weight at around eight kilos. This is what I did take:

Backpack 2000g
Walking poles 600g
Sleeping bag 800g
Micro towel 250g
Sandals 350g
Boots 800g
Socks x3 150g
Undies x 3
Bras x 2
Tshirt x 2 300g
Long sleeve top x1 200g
Light jacket 300g
Rain jacket 400g
Camera 400g
Notebook 400g

Spork
Bathers
Toiletries
First aid
Phone 300g
Guide book (John Brierley)
Air tickets, Passport
Hats (beanie & sun)
Sunglasses
gloves
Leggings
Divider bags 450g
Shorts 200g
Pants 300g
Water bottle 500g

Acknowledgements

Thank you Margaret Caffyn for publishing your book with my publishing house and supporting me in my planning for the Camino. Your friendship is precious to me and I love that you are currently living in Santiago to learn Spanish.

My family and friends were generous in gifting me money and gift vouchers to hiking shops to help me fund my gear for the trip: thank you Mama, Joe, Sara, Bill and Carole; my writing group: Michele, Mandy, Lynne, Carol and Kim; my book group: Dana, Heather, Louise, Kathy, Claire, Mandy and Kirstin.

To so many friends who followed my walk on social media and encouraged me every day.

Les Zigomanis for encouragement, a guidebook and helping to hold the fort while I was gone.

Most of all, to Kev for looking after the business while I was gone and encouraging me to do it while keeping the home fires burning.

To Dylan, Jack, Zoe and Oscar for looking after Kev in my absence.

www.ingramcontent.com/pod-product-compliance
Lightning Source LLC
Chambersburg PA
CBHW071729080526
44588CB00013B/1962